John Stephenson is an amazing and unique man who has expertise in so many areas. Aside from teaching the spiritual wisdom of Joel Goldsmith, he is also a sailor, surfer, artist, sculptor and scriptwriter. As one of the most committed individuals I know who lives and tastes life to its fullest, John Stephenson writes with authenticity, sincerity, honesty, inspiration and conviction . . . he truly walks his spiritual pathway.

For me, "Joy" has a higher spiritual dimensional energy than the word "Happiness" because "Joy" goes beyond the physical material dimension of what we call happiness. John approaches this subject with a depth of love that will inspire the reader to reach for what is available to each and every one of us. Is not the "Fullness of Joy" what we are all looking for?

GERALD G. JAMPOLSKY, M.D.
Co-Author of *A Mini Course for Life*

In his book, *Fullness of Joy*, John Stephenson, a truly inspirational teacher has given us the "keys to the kingdom." He clearly outlines the steps to a life free from physical limitation, financial limitation and emotional limitation. Can you think of a greater gift? I can't.

Thank you, John, we are forever grateful.

RAYMOND WAGNER
Motion Picture Executive

To know John Stephenson is to know someone full of joy, living a completely beautiful, peaceful, and satisfying life. Around him, others bask in the joy that radiates from his unconditional love – the greatest gift one can give another human being. He's written a brilliant, easy-to-read, insightful and inspired book with clear spiritual principles. *Fullness of Joy* makes it possible for anyone to experience unlimited joy – claiming their very own beautiful and satisfying life right now.

JEANNETTE PAULSON HERENIKO
President, Asia Pacific Films

In *Fullness of Joy*, John Stephenson writes from his own personal revelations and the diverse influences of many esteemed mystical teachers. The reader immediately understands that he is not simply rephrasing Joel Goldsmith, even though he sat at his knee as a child. This is instead a volume of fresh, spiritual inspiration – a departure from many post-Goldsmith pupils.

Just as Sufi mystic Vilayet Khan said, "... meditate on the stars to know the divine," John shifts the perspective and brings the stars to earth in a book that is straight from his experiences, reader friendly, and deeply touching. His personable, related teaching style is brought to *Fullness of Joy* like a conversation with a dear friend.

ANN MCCOY
Artist, Yale Lecturer in Visual Iconography

FULLNESS OF JOY

~

A Spiritual Guide to the Paradise Within

By

JOHN STEPHENSON

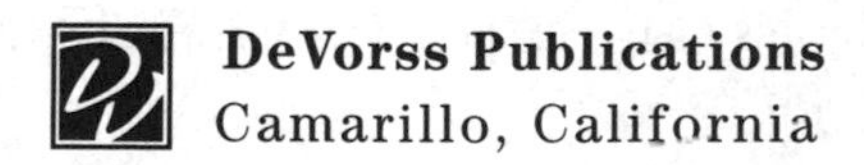
DeVorss Publications
Camarillo, California

FULLNESS OF JOY

ISBN: 9780875168708
FIRST EDITION, 2012

DeVorss & Company, Publisher
PO Box 1389
Camarillo CA 93011-1389
www.devorss.com

Printed in the United States of America

Library of Congress Cataloging-in-Publication Data

Stephenson, John, 1945-
Fullness of joy : a spiritual guide to the paradise within / by John Stephenson.
p. cm.
ISBN 978-0-87516-870-8 (pbk. : alk. paper) 1. Spiritual life. 2. Joy—Religious aspects. I. Title.
BL624.S7285 2012
204'.4—dc23

2012006188

DEDICATION

~

This book is dedicated to all seekers of Truth, especially my wife Sandra, whose commitment to the spiritual life keeps the flame of Truth alive in our house.

TABLE OF CONTENTS

PREFACE

~

I recently went on the web to search for "spiritual principles" to see what was there to bring joy and meaning to life. There were over three million sites. The first few pages of the search listed results like "six universal principles common to all people," "twelve spiritual principles and laws for the Aquarian Age," and "nine spiritual principles for getting everything you want." It made me think, "Is it necessary to add my voice to those who want to help people get what they want?" I realized that is not my goal. I don't want to help people in that way. My goal, dear reader, is not to help you get what you want, but to give you the tools to experience your spiritual self–the part of you that is one with God, inseparable from divine Joy and spiritual purpose, and always at hand. With that experience you will find bliss, and you will have the spiritual tools to lift you out of material limitations.

To experience the fullness of joy you need to know the universal principles that have brought joy to every culture. If you think of the Buddhist tradition, its purpose is to eliminate suffering from the earth. The principles that eliminate suffering are the same principles that bring joy to the individual. For the artist, the fullness of joy comes not in the beginning stages of learning the craft, but when the tools of the craft are second nature and the expression of the art is unlimited. A musician may love music in the beginning, and that love supports him through the learning period. But, the real joy of the musician is in expressing the music in his soul.

The principles presented in this book are the foundation for a spiritual way of life. They are based on my decades of spiritual study and experience. They come from every spiritual tradition and reflect the teachings of the great, illumined masters. They are meant to show you another way to look at the world; one that, when experienced, frees you from much of the pain and suffering that comes from having materialistic values. These principles lift you out of living from a personal sense of ego to living through your spiritual faculties.

Mystical principles are universal, and many masters have demonstrated them. Each master spoke, or now speaks, to his or her followers in the context of their parent society. With the insight to pierce the cultural cloak, and the ability to ignore the sense of time regarding the ancient masters, you discover that they taught the very same universal principles that have been given to mankind over and over again.

The following masters spoke to me and gave me insight into the Inner Kingdom:

- Krishna, who taught Arjuna the secret of seeing through the illusion of death into the spiritual nature of life, taught me not to fear death.
- Moses, who revealed the name of God, gave me the conviction to experience the true nature of God.
- Elijah, who took God out of the whirlwind, the fire, the flood and the earthquake, and revealed Him as the still small voice within, taught me to become aware of my inner resources.
- Isaiah, who taught how to reason from a spiritual standpoint, taught me the forgiving nature of God.
- Lao-Keun-Tze revealed to me that Oneness is a way to follow, not a goal to achieve.
- Gautama, the Buddha, showed me the unreal and powerless nature of physical effect.

- Jesus, the Christ, the great way-shower, showed me that death has no power in the presence of Christ Consciousness, and assured me that all can do as he did.[1] I accept the assignment.
- The Apostle John taught that God is love[2] – something I discovered as a child.
- Saint Paul instructed to have that mind which was in Christ Jesus,[3] and that is my goal.
- Rumi opened me to the ecstasy of oneness in movement and poetry.
- And from Mary Baker Eddy I learned that there is no life, truth, substance or intelligence in matter.

To all these great mystics from the past, the world and I thank you for the gifts you left behind.

I have also been blessed to know and study with some of the most noted twentieth-century mystics. Through their insight into the nature of the material world and through their healing consciousness I have benefited tremendously:

- From Krishnamurti I gained the discipline to remove all concepts of the appearance world from my perception and look at life without judgment.
- Joel S. Goldsmith opened my consciousness to the great I Am.
- And Virginia Stephenson, my mother, instilled the love of God in me and recognized and nourished my spiritual nature.

I am deeply grateful to all of my teachers, to those who have touched my life personally, and to those who left behind great spiritual legacies that continue to inspire me to live up to my spiritual potential and experience the joy of heaven on earth.

JOHN STEPHENSON
Kailua, Hawaii

What is Joy?

~

Thou wilt show me the path of life: In thy presence is fullness of joy; at thy right hand there are pleasures for evermore.

PSALMS 16:11

What is it that gives you joy? I was asked that question when I shared a draft copy of this book with a friend. In fact, he wanted to know the three most joyous things that I had experienced. I think that is a valid question for you to ask yourself. And what is the difference between joy and happiness?

One dictionary definition of joy is "something that is seen as a source of happiness." If I ask myself, "What is the source of my happiness?", I might have many answers: It could be my family; It could be my spiritual awareness; It could be my job or my talents. And, for me, it is all of those things. But, then I might ask, "What is the source of my spirituality, or my family, or my talents?" The answer to all of these questions is God. David's revelation in the Psalm quoted above gives us the same answer. Without God, there is no joy. We might have happiness or periods of pleasure and delight, but without God these experiences are transitory. With God we have the fullness of joy. With God we are tuned into infinite pleasure for all eternity. What a promise and what a revelation!

As we shall see, to experience this promise fully we have to know the nature of God. In what state of being was David when he wrote that psalm? When you read the whole poem, you see that David realized his spiritual birthright. The gods of this world do not satisfy, and with his trust in the Infinite Invisible he saw that he was maintained and sustained in and by Divine Consciousness.

So, on to sharing my most joyous experiences...

The first was my spiritual awakening. It took place on Maui in the summer of 1962. I was seventeen and had been studying the work of Joel Goldsmith, the great twentieth century mystic, since I was fifteen. I'd been to a number of his open classes and wanted to attend a week-long closed session in Hawaii. Since I was an avid surfer in Southern California, my parents, who were also students of Joel, were suspicious of my motives. Was I really serious about the class, or did I just want to go with them to Hawaii to surf? To test my sincerity, they made me a proposition. If I earned enough money with my after school job to pay for my airfare and class tuition, they would pick up my room and board in Hawaii. Actually, they had rented an apartment in Waikiki for two months that would accommodate all three of us. But, they had been to Hawaii before and had left me at home, so I took their proposition seriously.

I began to increase my work hours after school and on weekends. It cut into my surfing time, and I didn't go out as much with my friends during those five months before the class, but I was serious about this class. What my parents didn't realize was how much I had depended on Joel's books the summer before when I went to a military school.

Summer school at Culver Naval Academy seemed like a good idea at the time. I wanted to go to the U.S. Naval Academy for college and my parents thought the Culver experience would help. Also, my mom was nervous about me spending the summer surfing up and down the California coast. Something about sixteen-year-old boys, cars, and surfboards made her promote the military school idea with the fervor of a car salesman. So, I traded in my surfboard and California freedom for a lake in Indiana with a large variety of boats and a heavy dose of military discipline. The book that kept me sane that summer was *Practicing the Presence* by Joel S. Goldsmith.

The closed session in Hawaii was incredible. Hundreds of people from all over the world attended. Between sessions there was a tangible excitement, an expectancy of illumination that gave the student body a positive energy that I had rarely felt in large groups. During the classes there was the deepest of silences. Joel spoke for two hours every evening. In the mornings, students joined in meditation at the Waikiki study center. In the afternoons, Joel had two of his teachers speak. Eileen Bowden talked on the practical aspects of mysticism, and Virginia Stephenson talked on the mysticism of the Bible. In between these sessions, I surfed.

When the class finished, it felt like the universe gave a giant sigh. I know it was all taking place within me, but it seemed the whole island was more brilliant, more loving, showing forth more of the Kingdom of Heaven on earth. If you've ever experienced a spiritual healing–where the hypnotism of material belief lifts and you feel released from the burdens of the appearance, and inwardly there is a sigh of relief–that is the sense that seemed to permeate the island. The problems of the world dissolved (and the world seemed to be on the verge of nuclear catastrophe at that time), and everywhere you looked showed forth the glory of God. The sky was bluer, the surf more perfect, and the scent of the flowers was definitely more pungent.

A few days after the class, Joel traveled to Maui for a series of classes there. Most of the students from the Waikiki class had gone home, but a handful stayed on and followed Joel to Maui, including my parents and me. This was a much smaller class, maybe thirty to forty people, and Joel seemed much more relaxed. The Maui students welcomed us like family, and we shared in their humor, their music, and the gentleness of their "aloha." It was at this class that I experienced the deep nature of *I*. Joel's lesson was on the "I" – *I am that I am*. I don't remember what was said, but I'm sure that is common with that kind of experience. What I remember is the realization. What I had known intellectually was suddenly real. I am that I am. I went up to Joel afterwards because I think that I needed validation for my experience. I could barely speak, and Joel just looked at me and smiled. He knew. I've never felt such joy. Like it says in the Bible, "Rejoice, your names are written in heaven." That's how I felt.

The fullness of joy comes to all of us when we realize, as it says in Luke, "our names are written in heaven." In that Biblical story, Jesus had sent seventy of his disciples out into the world to heal in His name–meaning to heal in the name of I Am. They came back bursting with joy because they saw that evil has no power in the presence of realized spiritual consciousness. "Even the devils are subject unto us," they boasted. They felt the same freedom that I felt in my experience with Joel. The freedom of children of God is universal, and everyone who experiences their true nature experiences that freedom and joy. But, the Master clarifies their newfound state of being by indicating that the joy is not that you can heal on the human level. The joy is in the realization that you are one with God, inseparable from God's abundance, God's love, and God's glory.

The next most joyous moment in my life was when my wife, Sandra, agreed to marry me. In my eyes, she was, and is still, one of the most beautiful people on the planet, both inside and out. In answering the question, "What is it that gives me joy?", and in sharing my most joyous experiences, I realized that there was no *order* of importance in these experiences. *Every* experience of joy is a spiritual activity, and exists in the realm of oneness. Sandra and I met at one of Joel's classes. We became friends and discovered we had a lot in common. Besides our spiritual study, we both were artists. We had similar tastes in art, theater, and literature. We both loved the beach and the ocean. But, at the same time, there were circumstances that prevented us from getting married.

Over the years, I have seen many couples meet at spiritual events, who feel the unconditioned love that pours forth in that atmosphere and fall in love. They personalize that loving state of consciousness and attach themselves to someone in the group, believing that they have found their soul mate. Often, students fall in love with the teacher or guru. When they act on these feelings from a personal perspective, they can make a mistake. One couple I'm thinking of married after one of these spiritual gatherings, and later found that they had nothing in common on the human level. They had different ideas on how to maintain a home. They didn't like the same kind of food. They didn't like to do the same things. And, because they didn't have the depth of spiritual understanding to resolve these human differences *spiritually*, their marriage ended in divorce.

So, Sandra and I became close friends. We wrote screenplays together. We painted together. We both loved to cook and shared countless meals. And, there was our spiritual connection. Unlike those who immediately hooked up after a spiritual class, Sandra and I took our time studying the principles and attending meditations and spiritual classes together. Through this period, there was always in my mind the idea that we should take our relationship to the next level of commitment. I later realized that she had the same feeling. But, Sandra was divorced and a single mother.

The greatest obstacles in our spiritual development can be complacency and fear. If we get too comfortable in the way our lives are going, if we have a degree of success and harmony, we reach a plateau in our spiritual life and are reluctant to change. If we have grown attached to a certain way of life, to the good and comfortable things in life, and we are offered a change, we don't take it. Why risk a good thing even if it isn't what we dreamed of? But, joy comes in fulfilling our dreams. And, if we let fear prevent us from experiencing the fullness of joy, we become stuck at whatever level of spiritual realization we have attained…until the next opportunity comes along.

That opportunity came to me when Sandra wanted to move to Hawaii. I had given up on Hawaii. When I left Hawaii after returning from my voyage to the South Pacific (something I talk about later in this book), I had no plans of returning. My work was in Los Angeles, Sandra was there, and our lives together had reached a degree of happiness and fulfillment. We lived separately, but were together more than we were apart. And, now we both were faced with a choice. For Sandra and her daughter, Hawaii was the right move. For me, I didn't know whether to stay where I was or move to Hawaii. I had property and a good job in Los Angeles, and those were strong reasons for me to stay. I meditated on this. I went over it in my mind. To stay would be the practical choice, but then I'd have to let my love go. Or, I could let go of L.A. and start over in Hawaii. I chose love and Hawaii!

Finally, after establishing myself in Hawaii, I asked Sandra to marry me. She said "yes," and then asked me why it had taken so long. Fear was the first thing that came to mind. But, like most things that have a spiritual base, once you see through the human appearances, the obstacles or situations causing the limitations cease to have power, the grace of God comes in and makes the crooked places straight. At our wedding, my cheeks were cramped from smiling and laughing so much. Our life ever since has been a continual activity of Grace. We had the patience to develop a relationship based on spiritual principles. We knew each other, both humanly and spiritually. And, today, we continue to put into practice what we know of the Truth. We respect each other and exercise non-judgment. We see each other as equals, and celebrate the joys and successes that come to each of us as individuals, secure in our differences by realizing our spiritual oneness. And, we give each other the freedom to express life fully!

The fullness of joy brings with it an abundance that is not counted in possessions or bank accounts, but instead demonstrated in beautiful surroundings, harmonious relationships, and gracious living.

The next experience of joy on my list took place on a fifty-two foot yacht named *Tere* sailing back to Hawaii from the South Pacific. It came as the result of an experience I had of forgiveness. I tell of this experience and the power of forgiveness later in the book, but here I'll tell you about the joy that the experience brought. We were in our final days of crossing the Pacific from the island of Eiao to Hawaii. Eiao is the most northwest island and only a few degrees south of the equator in the Marquesas chain.

It had not been an easy crossing, and as we approached our home waters we were joined by a pod of pilot whales.

Pilot whales are closer to dolphins in size and appearance. They are jet black in color, with a short snout, bulbous forehead, and a sweptback dorsal fin set forward on their backs. And, they are about twenty feet long! We encountered over a dozen of these beautiful creatures off the south point of the island of Hawaii. We had a strong trade wind on our starboard quarter putting us on a broad reach in seas running with eight to ten foot swells. Every sail *Tere* could carry was up, and she was moving as fast as she could go, even surfing off the large swell. *Tere* means swift in Tahitian, and on this day she lived up to her name.

When I saw the whales, I went up to the bowsprit to get a better view. For those unfamiliar with nautical terms, the bowsprit is a short boom that protrudes from the front of the boat. Earlier that day the crew took turns straddling the bowsprit as the *Tere* surfed the swell, and as the yacht barreled down a wave she would bury her bow in the water right up to the bottom of the bowsprit. We'd lift our legs so the force of the water wouldn't push us off, and if the person at the helm was good, we'd rise again for the next wave without getting our backsides wet! But, if the helmsperson was off, we'd get drenched, and the force of the water would try to knock us overboard.

I don't know what sparked the next incident. Perhaps, it was the innate joy of life. The whales began swimming in front of the boat and playing around the bow wave, so I went out on the bowsprit and sat down to get a closer view. When I did, one whale riding our bow wave slid right under the bowsprit. As I rode the bowsprit down, I found myself right over the whale. Instead of lifting my legs, I reached down with my feet and rubbed the whale's back. It was such a thrill. I thought, "What a gift from God!" I assumed it would be a one-time event, but as soon as one whale swam away, another took its place riding the next wave. I shouted back to the crew so that they could see what was happening. From the deck, they saw the whole pod lining up like kids to ride the next wave and have their backs rubbed! This went on for a couple of hours. All of us on board – there were only five, including the skipper–took turns rubbing the backs of the whales.

What is joy? For me, it is watching the play of life in all its diversity. If we accept Jesus' admonition to be as little children, we will begin to play. We will see how joyous life *truly* is. And, when we know the principles that keep us in the Kingdom of Heaven, we experience the fullness of joy.

PART I

~

INTRODUCTION TO SPIRITUAL PRINCIPLES

Building Your Spiritual Consciousness

~

The Value of Spiritual Awareness

To come into the fullness of joy, we must develop spiritual awareness. Spiritual awareness is entirely individual. It does not depend on any guru, priest, minister, or teacher; and though teachers and gurus can lead you to the door, each one of us must step through it alone. The principles given in this book have been given in all the major spiritual texts of the world, but each presentation was in its own cultural context. For instance, the Old Testament of the Bible and the Vedas of India both describe a people's quest for illumination; the New Testament and the letters of Saint Paul showed the nature of Christ Consciousness; and Buddha gave the eight-fold path as a way to end suffering, while Mohammad revealed the five pillars to remind us of the oneness of God. The writings of Joseph Campbell reveal how mankind has forever been searching for the relationship between the unknown and the known, the spirit and the material. He linked the myths and beliefs of very dissimilar cultures and found a universal desire to know what is beyond the physical nature of life. Life has a spiritual component, and people around the world want to know their spiritual roots.

Throughout history, spiritual principles have been reiterated time and again. Frequently, spiritual revelations have been written down at the time and, thereby, preserved for future generations. But, more often it would seem that these universal truths have been interpreted and reinterpreted by every generation. Every generation has had those who knew the truth and have shared it with others. Some teachers or masters became very popular and famous, while other illumined individuals have shared their revelations to smaller groups and are only known by a few. The point is that spiritual truth is *always* revealing itself to mankind, and it is up to each of us to get in tune with this dimension of living.

Throughout time different masters have focused on different aspects of spiritual living. For some it was the way out of suffering. For others it was revealing the way of illumination–revealing the way to that conscious awareness of our spiritual nature within. And, still others focused on healing. Yet, all have revealed the impotence of material cause and effect to the individual with a developed spiritual consciousness. The common thread in all mystical revelation is an unseen reality–individually accessible through meditation–where evil does not exist, peace is realized, love is practiced, and joy flows to and from all who enter. When we live in this "inner kingdom," we live in the Master Consciousness, which expresses Itself[4] through us. The Master Consciousness, which is universal, lives out from Its spiritual center. As Jesus the Christ taught, the spiritual center is the source of the greater works that lift human consciousness out of the limitations inherent in the material concepts of life. You have that Master Consciousness within. It is what attracts you to a spiritual message and leads you to the teachers who can help you realize your spiritual nature and give you the tools to experience a life of peace, joy and freedom.

The purpose for understanding spiritual principles is to enable you to live through your Master Consciousness. To have a life that is free from physical limitation, financial limitation and emotional limitation requires a shift in perception from the outer to the inner. Our outer world is based on the dualistic belief in the power of good and evil, in material cause and effect. The illumined life is based on spiritual law. Saint Paul has a discourse in his letter to the Romans that defines the nature of spiritual law. Paul saw the difference between material law, in which good and evil are always in conflict, and the law of the Spirit that frees us from the material law of sin and death. Spiritual law negates all other law. To live under spiritual law, you must know its basis and the principles that constitute it.[5]

Our national laws are based on the principles that we all are created equal; that life is meant to be lived in a state of freedom; and that the individual can pursue happiness and fulfillment without interference from the state. In a similar way, spiritual law is based on principles that define the spiritual dimension of life. When you understand those principles, practice them, and when you exercise your spiritual birthright through inner realizations, you will experience spiritual fruitage. That fruitage is manifested as harmony, joy, fulfillment, and living a life without fear. Living under divine law reveals the ultimate reality of life and puts you in a state of grace.

Discovering Spiritual Principles

"Wrestle with the problem until the consciousness of the principle is attained." This statement, from *Living the Illumined Life* by Joel S. Goldsmith, got me thinking about the great spiritual principles of the ages. What are these principles? Is there a truth that, if realized, will bring spiritual freedom and joy? What actually constitutes the situations and conditions that limit our joy and fulfillment in life? Can those conditions be removed so that we experience the fullness of joy? Is there a way to be free of problems?

There is a universal truth–a set of principles–that, if understood, takes you off the wheel of cause and effect and reveals a Reality that has been with you since the beginning of time. Knowing these principles frees you from material limitation and reveals a creation based on love. Understanding these principles removes the seeming power of material problems. And, when you actually experience this Truth, you discover a freedom, harmony, and fulfillment that can never be taken from you. You discover a spiritual consciousness within that must be shared with the world, so that the world can come to discern Reality from the world of material appearances.

A *principle* is defined as "the primary source of something." Another definition is "the basic way in which something works."

In attaining the consciousness of a principle, you discover not only the source behind the manifestation, you discover how the principle works. For example, suppose you have a health problem and you ask, "Where is this problem taking place?" If you answer that the problem is in your body, or even that the problem is in your mind, you are on the level of the problem, and your struggle with the problem perpetuates it. If you solve the problem materially, you will not discover any spiritual principle, much less attain the consciousness of the principle. But, if you ask if this problem is part of spiritual reality, or if it is part of the belief in material cause and effect, then you have taken the first step in discovering the way Spirit works.

To resist anything of this world gives that thing the power it needs to survive. Buckminster Fuller talked about this idea in his book, *Operating Manual for Spaceship Earth*. He said that if two objects move toward each other on a collision course and they collide, both are destroyed. But, if they turn ninety degrees just before they meet, both are saved and neither has resisted the other. We can apply this to our daily experiences. If you don't immediately react, you can take a moment to assess a situation. You might ask yourself is there a spiritual principle here, a source to me that is not connected to my physical sense of self? Soon you are not dealing with a material appearance, but rather with the nature of who you are spiritually. You are Jacob wrestling with the angel, and you don't let go until you are blessed. You don't let go of the principles that define who you are until you gain the consciousness of them. Then you are blessed.

My teacher, the twentieth century mystic Joel Goldsmith, teaches in his writings that you can be *in* the world but not *of* it. Jesus the Christ taught the same thing to his disciples, but only after they had experienced the freedom of being in His consciousness. In Goldsmith's teaching, this way of life unfolds from the realization of your spiritual nature. Joel taught that a teacher might stimulate this realization, but in the end it is only your individual experience of the spiritual realm that brings the bounty, the glory, and the fullness of joy into your life. He taught that you have within you the capacity to live spiritually in a state of freedom and still participate in the world, enjoying the good, the beautiful, and the true without being subject to the suffering and pain of material law. This resonated with me.

Before I met Joel Goldsmith, I had a demanding concept of the spiritual life. I had to "stand porter at the door of thought," allowing in only those conclusions I wanted to bodily manifest. That was a heavy load for a teenager! The thought that I would suffer somehow from every carnal distraction that took me away from my spiritual self gave me great conflict. I wanted to have a good time, and I didn't want to feel guilty about it. I wanted to experience life, and not be cooped up in the mind where everything was weighed against metaphysical thought.

When I began to study with Joel, I experienced my spiritual Self in a new freedom that was not attached to what I held in thought. Thoughts no longer were power. In meditation I moved away from controlling thought into experiencing the silence of spiritual consciousness. In the class with Joel on Maui mentioned earlier in the book, I was lifted into a God experience. In a flash, I understood the mystical relationship of the Self–the "*I am that I am*" revelation of spiritual illumination. Later I discovered that that experience is universal and has been described by mystics throughout the centuries. The new freedom I experienced was not one based on material concepts or mental processes, but on my conscious oneness with God. The desire to expand that freedom has motivated me ever since, and the joy I have experienced in that freedom is a result of my spiritual awareness.

The spiritual life is not without discipline. In fact, it probably requires more discipline than living a humanly good and moral life. The spiritual life requires the mental alertness to see both material good and evil as two ends of the same stick. Spiritual freedom is not a license to do whatever you want, thinking that you are immune from the law of sowing and reaping, or karma. In the freedom of spiritual living, you no longer fear evil nor do you desire material good. You know evil doesn't exist in God and that God never created it.

I intentionally used the term "material" good because in the spiritual realm, there is a Good without opposite, a Good that is eternal and inseparable from the individual who realizes his or her spiritual nature. Evil is always on the material level because it does not exist spiritually. When you experience universal Good, you enjoy the pleasures of life without personal attachment. You see all good as an activity of the Divine, and the only thing that will limit your experience of that good is personalizing it. In other words, if you personalize your good by believing that it is coming from a boss, a spouse, or any material situation, that good is limited. What happens if you are fired? What happens if the financial markets collapse or your spouse dies? If you personalize good and that good diminishes, you will wonder what you did to cause that or perhaps you will blame it on God. However, spiritual discernment takes you out of that material structure and reveals the universal nature of boundless love. In that realization you can give up material desire in the knowledge that your spiritual nature is inseparable from God, and the grace of God is ever present in your consciousness. It shows forth tangibly in your life, to the degree that you become a transparency for that Inner Splendor.

The Way of the Mystic

Mystics know that the spiritual realm is experiential, not intellectual. Without the experience, you don't have the perspective to discern between spiritual manifestation and the material world. All mystical literature presents the idea of a spiritual realm and a material one. The spiritual realm is the Real, and the material is the unreal, illusion, or "*maya*." This is hard to reconcile when you see, hear and feel the material world around you. You may be told about this unseen reality, or as Goldsmith called it, the "Infinite Invisible", but it is not until you experience this unseen spiritual component of life that you have the courage to look at the material world and know that it has no power. A spiritual experience brings you into union with the

Infinite in the realization that you, in your spiritual core, are the manifestation of God. Every manifestation is unique, yet every manifestation is God in expression. Any conscious union with your spiritual Self that takes you out of the conceptual world, even for an instant, *is* a spiritual experience.

When you are aligned with the material realm, you are not able to experience the spiritual. When you experience the spiritual, you have a different perspective on the material realm, which removes the fear and desire that motivates human consciousness. Once you experience your spiritual Center and realize the significance of that experience, you see that the problems of life are not solved in the realm that created them, but instead are solved in spiritual Consciousness. Yet, you have not left "this world." You have gained the dominion of spiritual Consciousness.

Many religions teach that the only way to be free of human limitation is to die. The Abraham religions–Judaism, Christianity, and Islam–teach that if the believer has been true to the dogma and tenets of his or her faith, he or she will experience paradise after death. And since mankind has been unsuccessful in spiritualizing the material world, paradise is said to be some place "in the beyond" where the worthy are rewarded. Conversely, the evildoers suffer. Think about this: Isn't it a reflection of the human concept of karma, or "what goes around comes around"? Isn't it really the law of sowing and reaping and the desire for human justice? It seems that these teachings say that there is no end to that cycle, even in death. If you aren't punished for your mistakes here on earth, God will do it in the world beyond by sending you to hell.

This framework is the product of male dominated societies. It translates the omnipotence of God into material might and justifies the supremacy of man. It gives men the right to mete out punishment because in the embryonic stage of spiritual development, man saw God as an elevated state of himself. In the fog of the dream of Adam and Eve, man was created first and everything came under his domination. Very few civilizations in human history put the female, the receptive consciousness, in control. Usually the powerful dominant male consciousness dictates what is right and what is wrong. Even some concepts of paradise seem to benefit men more than women. For example, in the Islamic world, what does the idea of forty virgins mean to a woman?

But what if Paradise is here and now, and not somewhere beyond? What if dying doesn't refer to physical death, but to giving up attachment to material concepts? If we want to attain the consciousness of a spiritual principle, we must shift our perception. We must "repent," or change the way we look at the world. When you seek the spiritual life with the intent of knowing God *for God alone*, and not to get a healing or other personal benefit, you begin to step out of the orthodox relationship between God and man, and into a mystical relationship with the Divine. This relationship brings spiritual law into your life. You realize that you can experience the freedom of spiritual consciousness and, at the same time, live in the world. That is the goal of this book–to enable you, through the understanding and realization of spiritual principles, to experience spiritual freedom, even as you live your life in the world. In fact, that is the goal of all mystical traditions. It may be called "living in the world but not of it," or "walking the middle path," but the result is spiritual freedom and the joy that comes with it.

This is the nature of dominion. It is not a matter of power, but of spiritual awareness. When we begin seeing the world through spiritual consciousness, we see material cause and effect as impotent. Material conditions have no power over us because God is the only power, not a greater power than other powers. This perspective removes whatever fear we associate with a material appearance. We look at the world with a divine detachment in the realization that life is eternal and immortal. We realize that our individual lives are acts of divine love in infinite expression, and that sorrow, pain and suffering are not part of God's creation and therefore, not a part of us. A person can't change the laws of physics, even though that person may apply all of his or her might or brainpower trying. Apples will still fall from apple trees. The laws of aerodynamics will still govern the flight of an airplane. The rain will fall and the wind will blow, all in accord with the established natural order. But, an individual who is aware of his or her relationship to God *is a law* of peace and harmony to all within the scope of that consciousness. In other words, when someone experiences spiritual Reality in consciousness, only the manifestations of spiritual creation enter their world. Living in a state of freedom and joy is not about any personal sense of power over the evil of this world. It is about letting go of one's personal sense of ego and becoming a transparent extension for the activity of God. This is what we mean by "dominion."

In mysticism, we do not *overcome* material sense; we watch spiritual Reality replace material concepts. As William James said, "My experience is what I agree to attend to." When you direct your attention to your spiritual center, you open the door to spiritual Reality. The next step is to acknowledge the Spirit when you are aware of Its presence. From there you realize that the Spirit within is the universal grace of God. Grace then flows through this open door, and your life experience becomes one of peace and joy. It all begins with where you put your attention.

When an individual realizes this spiritual Presence and if storms threaten, the storms lose any destructive force as a result of the law of peace and harmony established in the individual's consciousness. Disease and conflict cannot exist in the consciousness of peace, and so they do not enter the experience of one who is in that spiritual consciousness. When you experience oneness with God, God becomes the spiritual authority over any sense of material power, not only for you, but also for all those in your consciousness. This is true dominion. It is not a force; it is not overcoming; it is not a miracle or something supernatural. It is spiritual law[5] having jurisdiction over material cause and effect, and it brings all earthly manifestations into compliance with universal principles. God is not doing anything to physical law. Dominion is the grace of God functioning through an enlightened individual.

The prophets, saints, and great masters from the past all tell us to choose between the Spirit and the flesh. What is this choice? If you choose Spirit, do you deny your human life? Or, can you be in the world but not of it? As you begin to understand basic spiritual principles, you start to observe human and material problems through the lens of spiritual knowledge. You stop trying to fix a world that the Eastern spiritual traditions call "illusion" or "*maya*." Instead, you expand your understanding of the underlying spiritual reality of the life you know. That spiritual reality exists right here and right now. You discover that God manifests *as* His creation, which is all good, and that anything God did not make does not exist, except as a concept in human thought. And, a concept has no power when the Truth is known.

Human belief is irrelevant to spiritual reality. The existence of God does not depend on what someone believes. God does not make the evil and suffering of this world, nor are they even known by Him. The mystic understands that God is "of purer eyes than to behold evil, and canst not look on iniquity,"[6] and refrains from trying to get God to fix something in the human dream. The way to freedom is to wake up! In orthodoxy we are taught that God knows our every thought and that the hairs on our head are numbered. This seems to say that God is intimately involved with our lives and that we need not fear the things of this world. This is true spiritually, but it is not true from a material perspective. The only way God functions in this world is through what is called Christ Consciousness: "I am the way."[7] The Christ is not a man, but the spiritual nature in all mankind. The Word is made flesh when an individual experiences the spiritual realm, or Christ Consciousness. Through that experience, the Christ activity of universal love reveals the truth, the spiritual Reality. As Jesus said, "Ye shall know the truth and the truth shall make you free."[8] And what is that truth? *I am that I am.*

There is No God in Material Cause and Effect

There is nothing to change or heal in God. God's creation is complete and fulfilled. If you are not experiencing the fullness of God in your life, it is not because God is withholding any good. It is because you have not developed the spiritual discernment to perceive that Realm. The reality is that there is only one creation. God is the substance of that creation, and God manifests *as* it. For the one who is aware of his or her mystical relationship with God, this illumined perspective nullifies material power. Both the Eastern and the Western traditions teach that it is an individual responsibility to know this truth, and that knowing this truth sets you free. Not only does it free *you*, it shows you the way to solve the problems of the world. Instead of wanting to change the illusory nature of the world, you bring into the world the universal benefits of spiritual wisdom, which manifest as new ideas in every realm–energy, health, caring for the poor and disabled, artistic creations of beauty and joy–all functioning under the spiritual principle of God as one.

To see the "unseen Reality," you must develop a degree of detachment from the world of human suffering and human pleasure. This is one of the most difficult steps in living between two worlds. How do you deal with the poor, the oppressed, the sick, and the dying? Turning your back on that part of humanity is not an option for those with love in their hearts. Yet, to accept suffering as part of God's world is not correct either. You may wonder how it is that an omnipotent God, who is supposed to be the embodiment of love, can allow suffering. It is because God knows nothing about the human condition. But, if that is the case, why have a god at all? Do you see how man created the orthodox concept of God from his own human beliefs and superstitions, and now expects God to control the world as some sort of super human? That "Santa Claus" god will never lift people from suffering because that kind of god does not exist.

God cannot be defined by human concept. God knows nothing of the hopes and fears of mankind because God did not create that level of consciousness. God's world is spiritual and without opposite. God does not enter the world of human belief because God never created it. Rather, man must enter into God's realm. When you enter the spiritual dimension, God is right there, even if you are living in hell! The moment God is realized in consciousness, human concepts melt away. The spiritual world, in all its fullness, exists right here, right now. To be in that world, which is a state of bliss, is to be free from the limitations of material cause and effect. Even though that "kingdom is not of this world," you can be in the world but not of it; you can be in the world, yet also be in "My Kingdom." It is all a matter of perspective.

In Buddha's time, the wealthy tried to hide the suffering of the world from their families–out of sight, out of mind. But, when the Compassionate One saw suffering, he wanted to find a way to eliminate it. In his quest, he discovered the powerlessness of all material phenomena. When an individual in the Buddhist state of enlightened consciousness witnesses an appearance of material power–either good or evil–the seeming effect of that power is nullified because that enlightened individual brings the dominion of Spirit to his or her world. And that "world" is not just his or her personal world, but also the world of everything that comes into that person's consciousness–even the activities of the person on the street, or an event affecting his community.

It doesn't matter what the appearance of power is. If it is the appearance of disease, the effect of disease cannot exist in the presence of an elevated state of consciousness. If it is the appearance of an attraction to destructive behavior, the attraction dissolves in this Presence. Buddha's great gift to the world was his discovery that human evil and human good are the same phenomenon, and that neither has power over anyone who is attuned to spiritual consciousness.

As the story goes, Gautama abandoned the austere practices he had been following to achieve spiritual understanding, and sat under a Bodhi tree vowing not to move until he attained enlightenment. Facing east toward the first light, he sat in deep meditation. Mara, the god of illusion and the personification of evil, came to disrupt his meditation. Gautama touched the ground with his fingers so that the earth could witness his path to enlightenment. Mara bombarded him with all the horrors of the world and could not get a reaction from him. Gautama continued his meditation, knowing the illusions had no power, and the weapons of destruction turned into sheaves of flowers. Then Mara sent his daughters, Tanha, Raga, and Arati (who represent desire, lust, and aversion) to seduce Gautama and break his meditation. The moment Gautama realized that everything Mara could produce in the way of human suffering or pleasure could not affect his meditation and his communion with divine Principle, he knew that Mara had no power. The moment it dawned on him that human good and human evil are one and the same, Gautama became enlightened. From that time on, he was known as Gautama the Buddha.

The idea that human good and human evil are one and the same is difficult for the materialist to accept because the materialistic view is that the world is built on material cause and effect. Put positive elements together and you get a positive effect. Put negative elements together and the result is destructive. Buddha's enlightenment repudiated material cause and effect and set a new standard for truth. Spiritually, truth is absolute and has no opposite. Yet, in the material world, "truth" is relative. For example, new scientific discoveries are continually replacing older ones that were thought to be "true." Even though the material world seems so permanent and set in its laws, that world can morph into something quite different at any moment.

Spiritual truth is the only universal and eternal truth. However, one cannot experience spiritual truth through the physical senses. The great masters teach us that there is a spiritual essence to individual being. Whether you call it Soul, Higher Self, Brahma, or Christ, Its existence is acknowledged worldwide in most cultures. Discovering the spiritual nature within puts us on the path to illumination. As we nurture receptivity to our spiritual center and recognize it as the Spirit of God within–not the God of Western orthodoxy, but the God that is the essence and substance of all that exists–and then realize our oneness with It, we experience a progressive expansion of spiritual awareness.

Spiritual Preparation

The practices necessary to make these principles relevant to our lives are ***meditation***, ***contemplation*** and ***prayer***. To gain the consciousness of a spiritual principle, we must take that principle into our awareness, contemplate it, and meditate upon it. Just thinking about a spiritual principle from an intellectual perspective will not give you the full experience of it. You may have an idea of the principle, but unless that idea is brought into action, it lies dormant in consciousness. The idea of aerodynamics came into consciousness during the Renaissance through Leonardo da Vinci. Perhaps it came to mankind even earlier, but it remained dormant in consciousness and only came into manifestation during the early twentieth century through the action of the Wright brothers. If spiritual principles are to be manifested in your life, they must be brought into action. An idea moves from the abstract into manifestation through the prepared and receptive mind. Therefore, you must contemplate and meditate in order to prepare your mind to be an instrument for Spirit. Once your mind is still, you are in the attitude of true prayer.

Mystical prayer is nothing like orthodox prayer. In mysticism, there is no outside power, person, or agency to pray to that will bring spiritual revelation to you. *Prayer, then, is not petitioning for salvation, nor is it seeking some blessing from an external power. It is the receptive attitude of listening to the Divine within your own being.* Prayer is finding that state of consciousness where fear and desire fade, and you come into a profound stillness and peace. It is the atmosphere of peace spoken of in the Bible. It is the "still small voice" of Truth that comes without words and thoughts, revealing the nature of Spirit.

Meditation is the path to "answered prayer," that consciousness wherein the nature of God is revealed. Meditation is not an end in, and of, itself. It is the means by which you bring yourself into a prayerful attitude. The main purpose of meditation is to move you out of the realm of words and thoughts, for which there are many techniques. Some traditions use mantras while others use breathing. I was taught to pay attention to the spaces between my thoughts and to refrain from attaching myself to my thoughts as they went through my mind.

I was given the analogy that thoughts are like vehicles on a freeway, speeding across my mind. Some of the vehicles were attractive, like classic convertibles or speedy sports cars, who pulled at me to take a ride, to own them, or to somehow become a part of them. Other vehicles were like working trucks that drew me to them out of a sense of duty. Still others were so ugly that they shouldn't have been allowed on the road. If I reacted to any of these images, I lost sight of the spaces between the thoughts and lost my receptivity to the Spirit. *When I stopped labeling and judging the thoughts, I lost my attraction or repulsion to them.* I could focus on the spaces between the thoughts, and thus become more and more aware of the spaces while being less captivated by the thoughts. When the thoughts stopped their parade across my mind, I entered that state of stillness, which is the atmosphere and attitude of true prayer.

The Gate to Illumination

~

I stand at the door and knock.

ROMANS 4:17 AND REVELATIONS 3:20

There is a great paradox in mysticism. The mystic acknowledges only the oneness of God, accepting that God manifests as the totality of creation and that God did not create evil. So, how do you reconcile all the various forms of evil you encounter in daily life? How do you deal with disease, crime, war, and hateful human behavior? Two of the great mystics, Gautama the Buddha and Jesus the Christ, taught that "this world" is an illusion and said to "resist not evil." Regardless of the appearance, God is functioning. We may not perceive that activity if we are wrapped up in the appearances of good and evil. That is why we do not contend with the forms of this world. It's not easy for the spiritual student seeking to live in God Consciousness to maintain his or her balance when confronted by the seeming power of evil. But, there is a way to avoid the grip of material power and to live spiritually and functionally in everyday life. It is a way that does not deny the duality of the material world, yet renders it powerless.

The structure of this world, discovered through human observation, is based on material cause and effect. Physics teaches us that for every action, there is an equal and opposite reaction. Ignite a rocket and it shoots into space. Everywhere we look in this world, we find a cause for every effect. If a cause cannot be immediately found, the "best and brightest" make every effort to find one. Evidence of this structure is found everywhere: A virus in the body causes illness; an insult causes anger; greed creates resentment; and, hate and fear cause war. The human psyche has been conditioned to react to these situations following the same belief in material cause and effect, which is *an eye for and eye and a tooth for a tooth.* Reward the good and punish the evil. This belief structure is not based on spiritual principle.

The basis of spiritual living is that God is the only cause and the only effect. If you accept the orthodox "Santa Claus" god described earlier, you fight the good fight, striving to be good, and you end up perplexed as to why this god sends pain and suffering to his creation or ignores the pain and suffering already here. Or, you do your best to avoid evil and hope that it doesn't touch you. The principles you are going to explore in this book are the tools that will enable you to see the non-power of material effect. You will learn the steps you can take to bring those tools into your individual experience.

The "gate" is a significant metaphor for entering the spiritual way of life. There are many instances in the New Testament where Jesus refers to this: "Ask and it will be given to you; seek and you will find; *knock and the door will be opened to you.*"[9] "Make every effort to enter through the *narrow door*, because many, I tell you, will try to enter and will not be able to."[10] "I am the way, the truth and the life; no man cometh unto the Father but by me."[11] In this last statement, Jesus is referring to the Christ, the I AM of individual being, the universal spiritual Self of all mankind. It is only through the activity of that Divine Consciousness within us or in the Buddhi mind that we discover the door, or the gate, and enter "My Kingdom."

The Buddhi mind (intellect in Sanskrit) is our higher mental faculty. It is different from the mind of ordinary consciousness and is our link to "atman" or the Greater Self, the Creator. In Christian scripture, St. Paul told us to have that mind which was in Christ Jesus. You can see how universal this is. *The state of mind that is non-reactive to the concepts of this world is the door to spiritual revelation.* It is a state of spiritual receptivity, which comes through meditation. It is not a product of material conditioning, but rather the result of our letting go of our conditioning, concepts, and judgments until we achieve a state of stillness and put our attention towards the spiritual realm. Actually, "My Kingdom," to which Jesus the Christ referred, is the conscious awareness of the presence of God. In that presence we experience the fullness of joy. We do not leave this world to enter My Kingdom, but while in the presence of God, this world has no power over us "except it were given thee from above."[12]

Imagine an allegorical portal, always at the edge of our awareness, etched with the principles that guide us on our journey from "this world" to "My Kingdom" and back. I envision this gate to be a Chinese "moon gate," a circle rising from the earth that is made complete when the individual enters. Living spiritually is a conscious act we all can make. We can stand in front of a door forever waiting for it to open, but it never will until the moment we reach out and grab the handle. In that moment, we have shifted from theory into action.

The mystical literature of the ancient Middle East was structured like a gate. A story, or parable, began on one side presenting its thesis or problem. The turning point was at the apex, like a keystone in an arched portal, and the other side of the gate showed how that transforming point fulfilled the thesis or resolved the problem. For example, the Hymn of Creation in Genesis I begins with God bringing forth light from the void and separating the light from darkness. Next, God made water and separated it from the sky. Then, God separated the land from the water and filled the land with vegetation–each plant and tree bearing seeds after its own kind. After three days we see the beginning of Life, but it isn't complete. On the fourth day, the apex brings the pattern of creation into view. God separates the day from the night, puts the stars in the sky, and gives us the sun to govern the day and the moon to govern the night. Now we have the pattern of life–the yin and yang of the whole–and all of it is good. The following days fulfill the pattern of life. On the fifth day, God brings forth the creatures of the land and sea. On the sixth day, He creates mankind, male and female, in his image. Lastly, on the seventh day He rests, for creation is complete.

So you could read the symbolism as follows:

- Illumination springs from the void of stillness.
- The environment for life is spiritual and universal.
- Life follows spiritual law.

The transforming event is time–the separating of day and night. It creates a pattern for this manifestation of life, a pattern of opposites that becomes the paradox for the mystic. In this paradoxical world, we see life take form and that form moves through time from birth to death.

- The animals appear in infinite variety on land, in the air, and under the sea.
- Man appears as God incarnate, male and female, both in the image and likeness of God.
- In rest, man finds illumination.

If we look at only one part of creation, the manifestation of life as seen through the physical senses, we might conclude that it is dualistic. Everything has an opposite. Everything exists in time. It is only when we see the whole that we realize that God is one, and that all creation exists in God, the timeless reality of now. In our rest, that is, when our mind is still and without judgment, we see this timeless reality and experience as the fullness of God.

For us to think in mystical terms, we must leave the linear sense of life and go back to the Oneness that poem reveals. The ancient story form always comes back to itself. To understand the mystical is to tune into the divine pattern that one is infinite, illumination is rest, and life is inseparable from its source. Life isn't about overcoming problems and accomplishing things to mark our progress from birth to death. It is a realization that all creation is One, and that the love that brought forth all we know exists within each of us waiting to be released.

This ancient way of presenting the spiritual aspect of life was sevenfold. In the ancient Middle East, the number seven represented completion. If you study mystical symbolism, certain numbers will stand out. "One" is the most significant because it is complete within itself. "Three" represents the trinity, which stands for the Source, Its manifestation, and the means or activity that brings about the manifestation. "Four" represents the Truth. It is the symbol of the earth with its seasons and the cardinal points of the compass. "Seven" combines heaven and earth. And, "twelve" is another number for completion. For example, the twelve tribes made up a nation, or the twelve months make up a year. None of these numbers have any power, but they represent patterns that remind us of the spiritual principles underlying all life. When we open the door, or step through the gate, we see the whole of creation, not just its expression.

As with everything in this paradoxical world, living a spiritual life–that is, being in the world but not of it–has two sets of disciplines. They are not really separate, but rather they define our approach to the conceptual world depending on where we are in consciousness at the moment. These disciplines are called by different names in different spiritual paths. To some, it is the absolute and the relative. Others call it the mystical and the metaphysical. In Goldsmith's teaching, he referred to them as the Nature of God and the Nature of Error.

Our gate, etched with seven principles like the ancient poem, has both the Nature of God and the Nature of Error. And, like the poem, our practice of these principles turn on the fourth position, Omnipotence. The principles that define the ***Nature of God*** are One, Now, Complete, Omnipotent, Omniscient, Omnipresent, and Unconditioned Love. To nullify the ***Nature of Error***, we practice impersonalization, non-judgment, detachment, non-power, non-reaction, de-hypnotization, and forgiveness. The key to dealing with error is seeing its impotence.

Moving through the gate in one direction, you have the principles necessary to detach yourself from the sense of power that the world of material cause and effect has on you. Moving in the other direction, you have the principles necessary to keep you from being hypnotized into believing that there is power in any form of matter. The movement between this world and My Kingdom is a matter of perception. The boundary between these states of consciousness is nothing more than belief–a universal belief accepted by mankind that material concepts are real and that they have power. That belief is false, and when it is seen as false, this world disappears. All that constitutes "this world" are concepts masquerading as power, and the idea that they can create and destroy is erroneous.

The journey from concept to *Is* is an individual one. Without a person, the principles are unrealized. They exist in consciousness but do not affect the individual, or the world for that matter, until an individual is motivated to step through the gate. From the perspective of the materialist, one may look at the gate for lifetimes, acknowledge its existence, and analyze and reflect on its beauty. But, unless that person steps through the gate, he or she will never experience the kingdom of heaven. From the perspective of My Kingdom, all one needs is the reminder of what constitutes Reality, so that the individual doesn't lose his or her way while in this world. When you experience what the principles mean, you understand that all is My Kingdom, and that this world and your experience in it conform to the spiritual realization you bring to it.

The natural man cannot enter the Kingdom of Heaven.[13] To step out of that "natural man" state of consciousness, we need to practice the principles that reveal the nature of error. They are healing principles. From the mystical point of view, healing is not the curing of illness or making our human condition better. It is the revealing of spiritual Reality to the individual. And, in that revelation, the individual becomes illumined.

Expanding the Gate

"Though seeing, they do not see; though hearing, they do not hear or understand. In them is fulfilled the prophecy of Isaiah: You will be ever

hearing but never understanding; you will be ever seeing but never perceiving. For this people's heart has become calloused; they hardly hear with their ears, and they have closed their eyes. Otherwise they might see with their eyes, hear with their ears, understand with their hearts and turn, and I would heal them. But blessed are your eyes because they see, and your ears because they hear. For I tell you the truth, many prophets and righteous men longed to see what you see but did not see it, and to hear what you hear but did not hear it."[14]

As this passage from Matthew suggests, illumination is a matter of perspective. Understanding the nature of error, and realizing the presence of God within us, gives us our freedom. We are healed by the spirit of God within, the *I* of our being, and we are blessed; we live by grace. Now, how do we apply these principles so that we can experience spiritual Reality?

Let's begin with the Nature of Error, which are the principles that change our perspective of this world. Also, let's start with the "keystone" or transforming principle, *non-power.* Seeing the impotence of material cause and effect is the key to stepping out of the limitations of material sense. What does that mean to you? Do you have enough spiritual insight to know that God is the only power? If so, you are ready to step through the gate, which metaphorically means that you are ready to begin to practice the principles that release you from material appearances.

Your first step is to see the *impersonal* nature of material appearances. Evil is the erroneous belief that there can be a power that contends with God. When you see evil as impersonal, you take away its power from the appearance through which it seems to operate. With that act, you can *forgive* that which appears to be evil. Forgiveness allows the activity of love to transform the situation.

Your next step is to release any *judgment* you have about the appearance. Judgment reinforces your belief structure–what you consider good or evil–and it *hypnotizes* you into *reacting* according to your belief. When you realize that God is the only good and turn over your concepts of good and evil to the Spirit, you have removed the power your beliefs have over you, and you have allowed the omnipotence of God to reveal the truth. In that sense, you have *de-hypnotized* yourself from acting out or being victimized by an erroneous belief.

In the third step, you become *detached* from human appearances, good or bad, and *do not react* to the things of this world. You no longer feel the need to resist evil because you know it has no power. You no longer desire the good of this world because you know that your fulfillment is in your realization of the presence of God, and that the grace of God will be ever manifested in your life.

In the end, you see how the principle of *non-power* (the metaphysical manifestation of *omnipotence*) transforms your perspective of life, allowing you to be in the world but not of it.

Knowing the Nature of God is knowing the truth that sets you free. The Nature of God is embodied in the seven principles stated above: God is One, Now, Complete, Omnipotent, Omniscient, Omnipresent, and Unconditioned Love. These principles make up spiritual law. If spiritual law is "I am that I am," what is the nature of the first I? It is the whole that is greater than the sum of its parts. It is your Being, and It is realized within you when you follow the ancient pattern of unfolding consciousness represented by the gate.

Again, the keystone, or turning point, is *Omnipotence*. Omnipotence has no opposite. It is the only power. It is not a power over lesser powers, nor is it a force that can be used for any purpose. It is a state of perfection, order, and harmony that universally functions in the smallest particles to the infinite reaches of space.

The Nature of God functions in us, through us, and as us in the following manner: *One-ness* appears as *unconditioned love*. That is, when we experience the oneness of God within, all fear leaves us and we love unconditionally. *Now-ness* appears as the *omnipresence* of God. In that moment of stillness and silence, we step out of the paradox of duality, of time and space, and experience the ever-present Nature of God. "Whether I make my bed in hell, thou art there."[15] What is there to fear? A God experience that is a realization of God's presence within is *complete*. Think of the Hymn of Creation–it is complete. From the void to the rest, all is complete. All is one. All is now. This manifests as *Omniscience*. Not only do we see the manifestation of creation, we also know its source and its substance.

As you put these seven principles into practice, you will find that you seem to move back and forth between a conscious awareness of the presence of God and the material perspective that deals with the appearances of good and evil. This is normal. The great masters did this and, by following their example, you can do it too. What it takes is mastering your personal sense of self through the application of these principles, in order to make your life an activity of Grace.

Here is the pattern of being in the world but not of it. It combines the metaphysics of the Nature of Error with the mystical Nature of God:

1. To experience *oneness*, you *impersonalize* the conceptual world through *forgiveness* and find your life empowered by *love*.

2. To live in the *now*, you recognize the *omnipresence* of God and that your life is untouched by human *judgment* and destructive material appearances.

3. Spiritual *completeness* wipes out your *attachment* to material good and you know the truth that sets you free.

4. When you realize the *omnipotence* of God, there <u>*is*</u> no other *power*. There is only the joy of Being.

Now you have wiped out material cause and effect and have opened yourself to the manifestation of God in this manner:

5. Wisdom, or *Omniscience*, will come to you in those moments of *non-reaction*.

6. The all-ness, or *Omnipresence*, of God reveals the spiritual reality behind the material appearance. If it is not of God, it cannot exist; the *hypnotism* of error disappears.
7. *Forgiveness* brings the fullness of *love* into your life.

Spiritual Healing

~

Incorporeal God, Incorporeal Man

You cannot separate spiritual healing from spiritual living. The more we live out from our spiritual center, the more harmonious and joyous our life becomes. This movement towards spiritual living changes our perception of the world, and those changes appear to this world as "healing." At first, it may be your attitude that changes, and your friends and family notice this. Perhaps you have physical challenges or are struggling with material supply. The more you let Spirit live your life, the freer you are from disease and lack. So, how does this work?

Spiritual healing is always approached from the absolute; otherwise, you tend to want to change some negative human situation into a positive one. The basic principle in spiritual healing is that God is All-in-all, creator of a perfect universe in which all that exists is a manifestation of the Divine, the spiritual. God has nothing to do with "this world" and the sooner we realize that, the sooner we stop trying to spiritualize something that is a material concept. Moses Maimonides taught that an incorporeal God could only create an incorporeal universe. He pointed out that idolatry, or entertaining some concept of God in one's mind, is the antithesis of spiritual law. Actually, the earliest of Hebrew law that prohibited worshipping physical idols was established to prevent the people from forming a mental concept to worship. The prohibition of worshipping physical idols was just the outer manifestation of this important commandment. The purpose of that commandment was to remind everyone that God is incorporeal Being. Without the realization that God is incorporeal Being, the idea of God's omnipresence degenerates into pantheism and leads man to believe that God can come down from heaven to change the human dream.

As all mystical teaching reveals, God knows nothing of the human condition. The human condition is the product of the collective belief in material power. God knows only Spirit, and since God is incorporeal, his creation (including man) must be incorporeal. Again, as Maimonides said, "...it is absurd to make images of God and to worship such images. Only under this condition can it become manifest to everyone that the only image of God is man, living and thinking man, and that man acts as the image of God only through worshipping the invisible or hidden God alone."[16]

To reconcile "this world" to the spiritual kingdom, which develops a healing consciousness, you must understand the "appearance nature" of material cause and effect. This begins with understanding the mind, something we will explore in more detail later. To begin to experience spiritual healing, you have to be clear about what spiritual healing is. *In essence, spiritual healing is your realization of the spiritual nature of life regardless of the material appearance before you.* Physicists, as well as spiritual teachers, have discovered that the human mind, in its universal collective state, is the source of all matter. When your spiritual faculties are opened, you begin to discern this. You begin to see that the material level of life is the product of this universal mind. You participate in the world of appearances according to your attraction to the appearances and the degree of power you give them. If you look at the world materially and try to bring God into it, you fail. When you try to bring Spirit into your mind with the desire to change some material concept, you fail. It is only when you let go of your attachment to mental concepts, and their material appearances, that you begin to experience the transforming activity of God within your own being. In that state, you experience the incorporeal nature of God *as* your individual nature. As that spiritual activity develops, you gain a degree of discernment and begin to act more and more as an instrument for spiritual revelation. Scripture calls this "the Word made flesh."

When you personalize this spiritual activity, you are no longer an instrument for spiritual revelation. If you have any personal agenda, even if it is the desire to heal the sick and bring peace to the world, you have lost the purity to be an instrument of God. Through your conditioned sense of life, your desire to change material appearances binds you to those very appearances by the fact that you have judged them in some manner. That attitude influences the events in your life according to your beliefs of good and evil. The idea that you are going to give the world your brand of spirituality because you think it is true will only lead to heartache and disillusionment. To be an instrument for spiritual awakening, your mind must be free of concepts so that, as Maimonides said, we can "worship the invisible God alone."

When you begin to see yourself as the manifestation of Consciousness, incorporeal Being, the material sense of yourself gives way to spiritual Reality. The more you can detach from your concepts about human beings–their structure, the causes of their ailments and behavior, and the changes brought about by time–the greater your freedom will be. What you think about yourself, and what you think about another, is universal in two ways. First, on the conditioned level, the basic material concepts of cause and effect are universal; they affect everybody. Second, spiritually, God is the only Self. Therefore, any sense of personalization hides spiritual Reality behind the veil of human concept, and any realization of your spiritual nature affects not just you but your whole world because there is only one Self. So, your first step in spiritual healing is to see through your spiritual faculty and release any identification you have with your conditioned state of mind and its manifestation.

The Nature of Mind and Thought

Mary Baker Eddy states in her writings, "Stand porter at the door of thought, allowing into your mind only those conclusions you want bodily manifested." In other words, watch what you accept into your awareness as true. The thoughts or ideas that come into your mind have no inherent power, but you can give them power by accepting as true whatever sense of cause and effect they contain. What you hold in your awareness (in your beliefs and your concepts) manifests in one form or another in your life. If you constantly visualize a Cadillac, and hold that image in your mind, you will probably drive a Cadillac. However, there is nothing spiritual about it. That kind of mental activity shuts down your spiritual receptivity. If you want to experience Grace and the joy that comes with it, you can make your mind a receptive instrument for God.

If you went to a hypnotist, the only power he would have over you would be in proportion to your consent. The only power an athlete has to "psych someone out" is in the perception one has of the other. Those less confident or fearful might attribute their failure to the mental power of their opponent, but that mental power has nothing to do with their opponent and everything to do with their own state of mind. You cannot use thoughts to change who you are because ultimately you discover that you are spiritual, beyond the realm of thought. On the other hand, you can become a victim of the beliefs and concepts you accept as power. So, you are instructed in your spiritual practice not to use thoughts–"right thinking" or affirmations–to change something. You are cautioned to use discernment, weighing the thoughts that come to you against what you know to be spiritually true. If there is no Truth to an idea or concept, then it has no power over you the moment you realize that.

The primary purpose for what metaphysicians call the "letter of truth" is to counter aggressive mental suggestion. When you can't immediately dismiss the appearances before you, you fill your mind with the truth you know about God. You might deny the appearance of power from a mental suggestion and affirm the omnipotence of God. But this is helpful only to take you out of the mindset of the problem and into the contemplation of the nature of God. The change in consciousness takes place when there is no more God *and* you. This requires the realization that God is impersonal and universal Being, not subject to the petitions and prayers of human thought. It requires being free from any orthodox concept you might still be entertaining about God. As you contemplate the oneness, the omnipotence, and the omnipresence of God, you begin to shift your attention from the appearance world to your spiritual core. Soon, the aggressive mental activities diminish and you enter the stillness, free of words and thoughts, where true prayer begins. In this state of consciousness you will have answered prayer.

Ego and the Mind

In mystical teaching, there is only one Ego, and it is God. God is the Soul of all sentient beings. There is not God *and* a person. The human ego, on the other hand, is the sum total of human conditioning. It is a compilation of the beliefs we hold to be true, the actions we take to do what we believe to be good, the actions we take to define ourselves, and the ever present fear that motivates us to protect and defend the concepts we have of ourselves or our loved ones. Our mind stores all this conditioning and it becomes the tool of our ego. The explanation of how all this works is a complex combination of brain chemistry and our thought processes. Without the awareness of Soul, we live through this mind/brain/ego as what St. Paul called "the natural man." To see ourselves spiritually takes a shift in our perception of mind and ego.

Your human ego is the conditioned concept of the one Ego, which is your spiritual Self, or the *I* of your being. The *I* of you is God, or in a more contemporary word, Consciousness. You can no more get rid of your ego than you can get rid of your mind or body. What you can do to become less egotistical is to begin to cut through the layers of conditioning until you see the spiritual nature of your ego. How are you going to see the truth about yourself except through your mind? Yet, if your mind is conditioned you will never see the truth. This sounds like the ultimate "Catch 22." But, notice that I have been talking about *your* mind, and *your* ego. There is a part of you that takes control over your mind and ego, since they are yours. That part of you is your soul, the individual expression of the one *I*, and the moment you recognize your soul as Spirit, you begin to shift your perception away from the conditioned mind into unconditioned reality.

Let's begin with your mind. What you think of as "your" mind is not yours; it is a universal mind. There is not "your" mind and "my" mind; there is only One mind. This mind is not contained in the brain. It has been recently revealed that the brain cannot store all the information available to us today and can process only a small amount of information at one time. Scientists have coined the term "outer mind" to describe this phenomenon. This outer mind corresponds to what C. G. Jung called "the collective unconsciousness." Metaphysicians call it "the conditioned mind." Therefore, all the information and experiences collected throughout the ages in this human experience reside in this one mind, and all human beings access it. As we begin collecting our individual experiences, they are added to this universal mind, and we categorize, or judge them according to our beliefs. We personalize them and make them our own. We notice universal traits in all people, and we agree to uphold a certain level of behavior to the benefit of all. As we give power to the concepts in this universal conditioned mind, we become subject to those beliefs, and they become part of our life's experience. As we personalize this one universal mind, we create our world.

Mind is also an instrument of communication. The wealth of information and experience stored in the universal mind gives an individual the means to connect to another. We draw on this vast pool of life to communicate our feelings and beliefs to one another. We justify our beliefs through the history stored there. And, as we realize the universal nature of mind, we see that it is one. We all have different perceptions of it, but when we discover that there is only one mind, that discovery opens to us a new world. We discover an instrument that connects us to all life.

The shift from the conditioned mind to the illumined mind takes specific steps. These are the meditative steps described earlier. The most important step is the realization that you have dominion over your mind and what you accept as true. If you accept material pretense as power, you fall victim to how that appearance plays out. If you reason from physical cause, you live out the results of that reasoning. You are the "I" who functions through the mind. And remember, there is only one *I*. As you recognize your true Self through the veil of your conditioning, you open the door to spiritual action. This spiritual action is Grace, and It begins to reveal the truth about who you are. It is the beam of light dispelling the darkness of human conditioning. You might not grasp what is happening to you when this first takes place, but it leaves with you the desire to know more about Spirit, to experience the presence of God, and to rest in Its bliss. As you go deeper into your Self, you discover that the *I* of you is God. It functions in you as the Master Consciousness, and you experience It as Grace. It is all One, and it is through your awareness of the unconditioned mind that you know this.

What was the state of your mind when you first experienced the presence of the Divine? Can you recall? If you can, your mind was probably in a state of stillness. When your mind is completely still, it becomes the means through which you commune with the Infinite. Your mind becomes the open door, inviting you into a consciousness of oneness where material concepts dissolve. You see your Self and experience the unconditioned Reality of life. This inner experience results in peace and harmony in your outer life. In fact, all of your life's experiences are dependent on your state of mind.

The mind is not creative. It is the door to the realm of Divine ideas. This realm of divine ideas, or cosmic consciousness, which

Deepak Chopra calls "the underlying field of intelligence that manifests as the infinite diversity of the universe," is the source of every new idea that comes into the world. You experience this realm when you see through the clutter of the conditioned mind. Mrs. Eddy knew this when she said, "The only logical conclusion is that all is Mind and its manifestation, from the rolling of worlds in the most subtle ether, to a potato-patch."[17] We live in the manifestation of the universal conditioned mind, which is a product of human beliefs. As you experience a still mind, you shift into omniscience and begin to live in God. There is nothing in the physical world that can tap into omniscience, that infinite pool of divine Consciousness. You access that realm only when your thoughts are still and when your mind becomes the open door to spiritual awareness.

At this point, you can see that the mind is a vehicle, a conduit of spiritual awareness. The mind is not the brain. The mind is not creative, in and of itself. The mind is not power, in and of itself. And, the mind is not God. Some metaphysicians equate mind with God, but this does not accurately define the function of the mind for the mystical student. God cannot be used, but the mind can.

Grace

When grace enters your awareness and opens you to the spiritual realm, it creates a desire in you to know more about this facet of life. It motivates you to learn how to rightly meditate and pray. And, as in all disciplines, there are some basic rules for entering the spiritual realm. The first one is that your motives must be pure to reach your spiritual center. There can be no desire for personal gain if you are going to grow spiritually. That's part of the great paradox: "To gain your life you must lose your life."[18] The second is that in the stillness of meditation, you cannot direct good to anyone. Sending good thoughts to someone suffering does nothing for the person suffering, and it prevents you from fully experiencing the oneness of God. If you think there is God *and* you *and* another, you are not in the spiritual realm. Finally, meditation is not the goal; it is the means. Through an unconditioned mind, your goal is to know the deep silence that is the atmosphere in which you experience the presence of God, which is true prayer. The mind is still. You are Being, not doing, and in this state of consciousness, you are the manifestation of God. Then your action becomes an activity of universal Good.

When you realize that God is the Soul of man, and if you are pure in that realization and make no image of God or direct some supposed "God power" to anything, then you will experience Oneness. Through the purification of your mind, you dissolve the sense of separation that believes there is God *and* man. The mind is the vehicle that takes you to this realization. You do not end up in the mind; you come into the union of Soul, in the realization that your Soul is infinite and eternal Being. The experience of Oneness is answered prayer. Answered prayer appears as the Grace of God flowing through you and touching all within the scope of your consciousness. All of this takes place in the realm of Soul, beyond words and thoughts.

"Let this mind be in you, which was also in Christ Jesus: Who, being in the form of God, thought it not robbery to be equal with God: But made himself of no reputation, and took upon him the form of a servant, and was made in the likeness of men:"[19]

The personal ego knows nothing of that mind which was in Christ Jesus. All it knows is itself, which is based on human conditioning. The personal ego judges concepts based on its own belief in good and evil, and it tries to reconcile that belief with a benevolent, omnipotent and omniscient deity. That cannot be done. God cannot be perceived through the conditioned mind. The rewarding and punishing God that is put forward by most orthodox religions in an attempt to make people humanly good has nothing to do with spiritual life. Orthodoxy says that man was given free will and that he has a choice between good and evil. The mystic knows that until you awaken to your spiritual nature, you have no free will. As a human, you have given your dominion over to material cause and its effect, and to the resulting beliefs in good and evil. The human perspective of life has forsaken the relationship you have with the Truth.

The Paradox of Mind and Ego

In the competitive world, we all seem to struggle with our mind and ego. The mystic knows that there is only one Mind and one Ego. You don't have a God mind and a carnal mind. Your ego is not a self-centered attitude seeking gratification. It is not something you need to get rid of or control in order to be spiritual. That is a concept of ego seen through material conditioning. There is not an ego *and* you, or an ego *and* God. There is only One! But, that mystical revelation can be fleeting and hard to recall when trying to get ahead in the world. Even if you intellectually know the principle of oneness, to experience oneness as part of your everyday life takes discipline. It takes daily meditation to keep God in your consciousness so you can begin to see that there is not really this world *and* My Kingdom; there is only My Kingdom. Another paradox in mystical living is that our mind and ego function both in the world and in spiritual Reality.

When you are touched by the stillness in meditation and experience a quiet mind, your perception of yourself begins to change and you start observing your mind and ego from the perspective of spiritual oneness. When you function from the conceptual paradigm based on the belief in the power of material good and evil, you experience what is expected from that way of looking at life. After you become aware of your Soul faculties–that part of you that can be detached from the conceptual world–the same mind and ego that interpret the appearances of this world shift and you begin to see things differently. The mystical way of life (which is a result of our experiences of oneness) sees through the fear that comes with negative appearances and is not easily drawn into the physical pleasures of good appearances. Again, we see that this is the middle path. Our spiritual awareness, consciously entertained, takes us away from the battle of conflicting forces and brings us under spiritual law. Our mind and ego are the same mind and ego, but they now serve as instruments of Soul. There appears to be two worlds, but in reality they are just different perceptions of the one. One perception is a material perspective that puts us under the laws of matter, and the other is a perspective from Soul that puts us under spiritual law.

Recently, at the University of California at Santa Barbara,[20] researchers did experiments to find out where the quantum world broke down and the classical world of physics took over. For those unfamiliar with these disciplines, quantum physics studies the behavior of atomic and subatomic particles, and classical or Newtonian physics studies and measures the physical world. In the quantum world an object can be in two places at the same time, something impossible in the physical world. In this experiment, the researchers wanted to find out how large an object could be before it shifted from quantum law to Newtonian law. To illustrate this idea, the interviewer asked the scientist a hypothetical question, "Could my boss be in his office behind a closed door and not in his office at the same time?" The scientist said it was possible if his boss was "poorly coupled to his environment," and that if the interviewer wanted to test this by opening the boss' office door, that would force his boss to choose whether he was in his office or not. In other words, our attempt to measure the quantum world forces something in that world to be either energy or a particle. Under our observation, it can't be both at the same time. The experiment did find that something the size of a human hair can behave in the quantum way. The question now being asked is how influential the quantum world is on the physical world.

The mind/ego paradox is much like the relationship between the quantum world and the physical world. When you see the physical world through your soul-infused mind and ego, you see not only the objects of this world, which are colored by your conditioning, but you perceive the spiritual reality behind the appearance at the same time. You see the "word made flesh," or God in manifestation through the unconditioned mind. You experience this in the *now*, and in that *now* moment, the fullness of God brings you under divine law. The result of this is that objects in the physical world that have no spiritual substance cease to exist. In this sense, "objects" are not necessarily things; they can be ideas, relationships, and situations. A hypnotic suggestion cannot manifest itself, so the objects of material sense–the appearances formed out of human concept–disappear from the experience of an illumined individual. You don't have to be a Buddha or a Christ to see this. To the degree that you live out from your Higher Self, you will see your world conform to divine law. If the material picture is based on a concept built in the conditioned mind and personalized ego, it disappears when you are under divine law. As the observer, the one measuring and testing your world, you bring about your experience. In this world, you are constantly measuring and testing one concept against another. In My Kingdom, you are in the *now* where infinity is the measure.

Your mind and ego (in their conditioned state) work to convince you that what you see through them is true. This combination of mind and ego can manipulate you into accepting and acting upon what fits your preconceived reality. You probably know someone who manipulates the truth of a situation so that good intentions appear bad. The suffering is blamed on the innocent victim, who is made out to be the evil one. A thief attempting to rob a store fell through the skylight of the store and sued the landlord for his injuries. He claimed the landlord was negligent for not having safety bars over the skylight, and the thief won damages! In the same way, the conditioned mind manipulates the truth to boost the personal sense of ego, or to protect the ego from embarrassment or blame. Through the conditioned mind, you see what your concepts want you to see based on your beliefs and conditioning. Good and evil are relative to your conditioning. As long as you function from the perspective of this world, you are a victim of the world's beliefs. The moment you realize that you have another avenue of life, one based on spiritual principle, you are free from the slings and arrows that the personal sense of ego throws at you.

Your personal sense of ego depends on the concept of self-preservation for its survival. All creatures supposedly have this mechanism, and in humans it is heightened by self-awareness. It is said that we are the only species to have self-awareness; other species function completely through instinct. To a degree, we have the same protective instinct in the face of danger as other species do; that is, we either flee or stand and fight. As our reasoning faculties come into play, we adjust that reaction according to our past experiences. But, to experience the freedom of God consciousness now, you need to enter into Master Consciousness within and bring yourself under spiritual law. That law is succinctly defined in the Master's Sermon on the Mount. Basically, it says that you do not resist evil, you do good to those who persecute you, and you forgive "seventy times seven."

Another way to look at the mind/ego relationship is to look at it as you would a computer. Computers communicate and execute processes using ones and zeros–off and on, if you will. You could say that a "one" is something and a "zero" is nothing. These two elements work to create a virtual world. When you look at that virtual world on a computer screen, it almost appears real. You can communicate in it, play in it, and be informed by it. You might even talk to your computer as if it was something cognitive and creative. Then, you realize that there is nothing behind it but ones and zeros. The creativity you see on your computer screen is the product of the person who created the program. Remember, the paradox is that we have a sense of duality that appears as "this world," when the reality of life is One.

You relate to this world either through the conditioned mind, which is the personal ego perspective, or through your awareness of spiritual reality. When you remember that the architect of creation is Consciousness (the Infinite Invisible, your Soul) you no longer give power to this world in the same way. You are in the world in an unconditioned state. In that state, there are no concepts and beliefs; there is no time and no space. The unconditioned mind is a pure state of receptivity for Omniscience, the divine wisdom. When you view the world from the conditioned mind, you make a reality out of your beliefs. Thoughts and ideas manifest themselves through human action into the things of this world. When you see the world through your developed spiritual faculties, God is the only reality–and you cannot have a concept of God.

Your mind has two modes, conditioned and unconditioned. You are all too familiar with the conditioned mode. It is the state of mind that makes you react to world appearances and puts you on the emotional roller coaster of pleasure and grief, and fear and security–all of the feelings that define your personal sense of self. The unconditioned mode of the mind appears in meditation. It is a state of being that is beyond words and thoughts. These two modes, the conditioned and the unconditioned, alternate in our awareness. The conditioned mind builds the personal sense of ego, forming our personality. The unconditioned mind reveals our spiritual Self and brings us under spiritual law. Both of these are always working in us. Because the universal concept of life is a material one, you only become aware of the unconditioned mind through a spiritual experience. Once you are aware of the unconditioned mind, you want to know more about it, and thus your spiritual journey begins.

To the degree that you let go of your human beliefs, you enter the unconditioned state of mind. You can use the tools of metaphysics to help you detach from your human beliefs. You have what is called the "letter of Truth" to release your attachments to material concepts and experience the oneness of God. The freedom that results is a state of unconditioned "nowness" that manifests through you to meet your every need. The more you are attuned to this state, the more it functions in your life. In a sense, you have "one," the conditioned state of mind, and "zero," the unconditioned state of mind, functioning within you at the speed of *now*. At any moment, the processing of life can shift from the material to the spiritual. Erroneous materialistic beliefs (which derive a sense of power from the universal acceptance that they are something) bump up against the spiritual reality of one Cause and disappear. This happens instantly as Spirit flows through the unconditioned mind. Just as light dispels darkness, Spirit reveals to you the reality of your world as it is in God.

The more you know and experience the unconditioned nature of life, the closer you are to God and Its manifestation. The more you

Please note that the sentence on page 54 continues onto page 55.

We are aware of this and hope it does not disturb your reading.

Please accept our apologies for this inconvenience.

~The Editors

Our Spiritual Axis

~

Mind demonstrates Omnipresence and Omnipotence, but mind revolves on a spiritual axis and its power is displayed and its presence felt in eternal stillness and immovable love.

MARY BAKER EDDY

experience the unconditioned state of mind, the less the conditioned mind influences your life.

What does it take to experience the presence of God? It takes a mind not wrapped up in judging life, in judging your friends or your situations. It takes a willingness to step out of that pattern of life and let the spiritual realm come into your awareness. Someone with a strong mind and strong concepts of what constitutes good and evil usually has a strong personal ego. That is, they project a personal sense of power backed up by what they know. In the East, this kind of ego based on personal power is likened to the coconut. The outside of the coconut is covered by layers and layers of tough fiber. Normally you need a tool of some kind to help strip off that fiber. Once the fiber is removed, there is an even tougher shell. One needs to get through those barriers to get to the meat and the water, and all the nutrition inside.

I once attended a coming-of-age ceremony given by a guru after an initiate had completed the initial steps in entering the spiritual life of the ashram. The guru explained the metaphor while holding a shelled coconut. He had already peeled off the husk, saying that it was like the layers of the mind filled with the beliefs and ideas accumulated over the years. All those beliefs and ideas protected the hard shell, which represented the ego. That personal sense of ego is laid bare when the mind lets go of its concepts. The guru picked up a hammer and began tapping the coconut on its ribs. "It is the activity of Truth," he said, "that cracks open the ego." When the concepts are gone, spiritual reality is revealed. That spiritual nature acts like the hammer. It knows where the weak spots are and gently taps them.

The guru kept turning the coconut in one hand, while tapping it with the hammer in his other hand. Sometimes the coconut opens quickly, and sometimes it does not. And, you don't want to smash the coconut because you want to use the two halves of the shell to hold the water. As he was talking, the coconut suddenly split into two perfect pieces. The guru held them up, spilling only a small amount of water. He then said that when the ego lets go, the purity of the soul is revealed. Now, you may ask, are the husk and shell and meat separate? No, they are all the coconut. They are one. But, where is the power of the coconut? It is in the meat and the water. They have the life giving properties.

In Polynesian societies, the coconut tree is the tree of life. Everything on the tree gives something to the society. The people thatch their houses with the fronds. They lash the framework of their houses with rope made from the fibrous husks. The meat and the water are food staples. When a boy asks for a drink of water on a beach lined with coconut trees, the man tells him to look up.

Now, imagine the purity of the soul within you. It is inseparable from the wholeness of God. In fact, the mystic soon realizes that God is the soul of man. This is our spiritual axis. Around this is the ego and it is inseparable from God. There is only one I, and our mind is the instrument that can reveal the ego and open "out a way whence the imprisoned splendor may escape."[21]

The Imprisoned Splendor manifests Itself in many ways. For Moses, it was the voice that came from the burning bush that did not consume itself–a powerful symbol of life manifesting physically, yet existing in spiritual illumination. Moses realized that all life is God. *I am that I am.* That is the essence of spiritual law. When the spiritual realm is as real for you as it was for Moses, your opened spiritual nature will define how you live. You will then have the tools to nullify the material power of this world just as Moses nullified the power projected by Pharaoh and his priests.

In the Western world we have our own symbols that define our state of spiritual realization. It is a trinity that far precedes the orthodox trinity of Father, Son, and Holy Spirit. It began as father, mother, and child–seen in its perfect union and transferred to earth as the nuclear family. But, it is more than that. It is the complete expression of life. Father, mother, and child are one life functioning in their primary expressions. They represent the unity of life, and when the esoteric (the inner) melds with the exoteric (the outer) you have heaven on earth. That is the sublime vision of mysticism–experiencing the joy and freedom of spiritual expression without the limitations and suffering of material belief.

The Holy Trinity of Father, Son, and Holy Spirit are manifested individually as body, mind, and soul, where the Father is the soul, the Son the body, and the Holy Spirit the mind. The spiritual axis always connects the Soul and the Father, for they are one. For the mind to demonstrate the omnipotence and omnipresence of God that is displayed in eternal stillness and immovable love, it needs to be free of the material concepts that bind it to this world. The act of grace that frees the mind does not take intellectual might or thinking power; it takes a willingness to let go of the material thought process so that the mind becomes an instrument for the Divine. The mind enters a state of stillness. In that state of consciousness, the body becomes the Son and the individual functions under the law of God.

The union between the higher trinity–Father, Son, and Holy Spirit–and the lower trinity–soul, body, and mind–is our spiritual journey. In all esoteric teaching, this union takes place in three degrees or three steps. This first step is the awakening to the spiritual realm and its relevance to one's life. If you live just on the lower trinity of soul, mind, and body, without awareness of your spiritual axis, you are what St. Paul called "the natural man." The moment you become aware of your soul connection, you begin your spiritual journey.

The transition from your worldly state to a state of Grace follows the specific path the great masters have forged for you. The path begins with identifying your soul as the Infinite Invisible within, rather than with the personal sense of "I," which is your ego. You have a spiritual axis that unites you with your Source, and this axis can never be broken. Some have referred to it as the "golden thread." When you achieve a degree of illumination, and let go of your human conditioning, you become aware of your spiritual axis. However, until you accept the reality of your being as spiritual, you will be praying amiss.

Human Nature

St. Paul teaches that the natural man cannot receive the gifts of the Spirit. Today, we would say that the "natural man" is the state of consciousness that is not aware of any transcendent faculty, and has not experienced mystical union or perceived that there might be more to life than what can be seen, felt, and measured. The natural man believes that God and man are separate. He might accept the orthodox Holy Trinity of God the Father, God the Son, and God the Holy Spirit, but he can see no relationship in it with himself. He believes his mind is separate and personal, and he believes his body has no relationship to Spirit. Although the spiritual axis exists in him, as it does in all people, he has not found the "link" within him that reveals it. He functions in the world from the basis of universal conditioning, which is the collective belief structure of humanity that forms our conceptual world. Fear and desire motivate his behavior, and his ego is in the driver's seat. This individual lives on the lower trinity, subject to all the variables of material cause and effect, until there is an opening in his or her consciousness. These people can even be religious, but until they grab hold of their spiritual axis, they will not experience the presence of God.

To be an instrument of God, you need to know how to get out of the way humanly. As Mrs. Eddy said, "Error once seen is two-thirds destroyed, and the other third destroys itself." What is "error"? In the context of mysticism, it is the sense of power that we give to material beliefs. That power does not come from God. It is generated by our ego-mind and affects our concept of body and the world around us. A giant step out of the limitations of this world and towards living from our spiritual center is the ability to see material appearances as impotent. Once we have done that, we can let the appearance go, in the knowledge that God is the substance of all creation. If it is not of God, it ceases to exist, or using Mrs. Eddy's term, "it destroys itself." Nothing of God is *ever* destroyed. The only thing that can be destroyed is the false human concepts that are generated by the belief in good and evil.

The false concept of our relationship to deity is like this:

1. Instead of the Soul as God incarnate, there is God *and* the individual. This creates a sense of dualism and produces fear and desire.

2. Instead of mind as a transparency for God realization, there is the ego/mind that personalizes fear and desire.

3. Instead of incorporeal body, there is the manifested ego seeking material fulfillment and fearing death.

The basis for the conditioned mind is the concept that your soul has fallen from grace and is looking for redemption. As a race, we have rejected our spiritual birthright and created a world of duality. This is what the allegory of Adam and Eve depicts. On the universal level, the conditioned mind violates all the great spiritual principles.

1. The conditioned mind cannot accept *oneness*. How can an incorporeal God be one with a mortal body?

2. The conditioned mind does not attest to *nowness*. We all

know about the past, and project our future from our experience of the past.

3. The conditioned mind is not *complete*. It fears evil and desires good, which it sees as something outside itself in the world to be taken.

4. The conditioned mind is not *omnipotent*. Who by taking thought can add one inch to their stature?

5. The conditioned mind is not *omniscient*. It can only project from concept.

6. The conditioned mind is not *omnipresent*. It functions through a linear process.

7. The conditioned mind does not *love unconditionally*. It is the root of opposites–loyalty and betrayal, reward and punishment, affection and hatred, war and peace.

You can see how human conditioning alters your awareness of spiritual Reality. When you realize that you have a spiritual axis and are never separated from God, which is your Soul, you begin your spiritual journey.

The Illumined Individual

The person living in an illumined state of consciousness has discovered that he or she can experience the presence of God through an unconditioned mind; that is, a mind free of personal judgment and free of any concept of the divine. This is the second step in unfolding spiritual awareness and it eliminates the sense of separation the natural man feels from the spiritual realm while in the material state. In the moment of spiritual revelation, we leave behind human perception and begin to see the world more through our spiritual consciousness. We begin to see the spiritual substance of all form, while the attachment to the personal sense of life (the human ego) diminishes until we are pure transparencies for the activity of love in the world. The mystical symbol of this unfolding awareness is the coming together of the two trinities. They make a square, the four-sided symbol of Truth.

In the illumined level of consciousness, eternal life–the Godhead–is experienced in the soul, for God is the soul of us all. When you have this experience, you are fully conscious of spiritual reality. There is no separation between what appears in this world and the source of all life. The trinity of expression is united with its source, and the Life, Truth, and Love of the Spiritual Trinity function through the unconditioned mind and a body of love. You know the truth from a Soul experience. It isn't the truth that frees you. It is your *individual knowing of that truth* that frees you. Once you experience that truth, no amount of material conditioning can alter it. In this illumined state, where the mind is a pure transparency for the Divine, the truth about God is realized. You realize that your body is a body of love. Your body is the temple of God, and becomes the instrument of love, love in action in this world. This love is not personal. It is universal, without the language of personal sense. Where divine love is present, there cannot be pain and suffering. Where there is unconditioned love, there cannot be hate. You have moved out of the realm of dualism with its opposites into the consciousness of spiritual union. Here all is one. Eternal Life is your individual soul. Spiritual truth is the law of that land. What is spiritual truth? It is the reality of spiritual creation manifested, and the vehicle, or body that carries this to the world, is love.

The Transcendent Individual

This state of consciousness is mystical union. It is the final step in spiritual awareness. The "reflective trinity" has merged with the "source trinity" until they are completely intertwined and one. The six-pointed Star of David symbolizes this. A person who experiences union is complete. In moments of deep silence, where you lose all attachment to the physical, you know God aright, "whom to know aright is life eternal."[22] This state is Christ Consciousness. It is the Word made flesh: "Even in my flesh shall I see

God."[23] In this union, you know your soul to be omnipotent. This awareness dissolves all sense of material power, for matter cannot coexist with Spirit; and in this state of consciousness, you are Spirit. Omniscience (all-truth) comes into the world, for your mind has been purged of its material concepts. Can your mind still function on earth? By all means, yes. It is the mind that was in Christ Jesus; it is the Buddhi mind, or Atman. It sees through all material appearances to the spiritual reality that has existed since the beginning of time. There is no process in this recognition. There is just the immediate knowing of spiritual manifestation, for this experience does not take place in time or space but in Consciousness. It is carried to earth in the ever-present manifestation of the image and likeness of God.

Alas this is the full circle, the alpha and omega. Your understanding of these degrees of spiritual awakening motivate you to walk the spiritual path, even though the appearances of this world seem so real. You step through the gate, embracing the principles necessary to lift you out of the conditioned life. You step back into the world practicing the principles that keep you in heaven. You begin to live in the world but not of it. The joy you experience takes on a new perspective. No longer bound by human conditioning, you are free in the infinite flow of universal bliss.

As you continue through this book, ponder each principle. Take each principle deep into your consciousness until you have an experience with it. Your experience has nothing to do with what is on the page and *everything* to do with your receptivity to Truth. Everyone has spiritual faculties, and these faculties are as much a part of your being as your senses, emotions, and intellect. When the awareness of your spiritual nature is ignited in you, it opens you to a new world.

PART II

~

SPIRITUAL PRINCIPLES

The Seven Great Spiritual Principles

The seven great spiritual principles represent seven aspects of the Divine. All are part of the God-Experience, and none can be divorced from God. These principles are the foundation of spiritual law. As I said earlier, spiritual law is "I am that I am."

The "I" that is God functions through the "I" of the individual as spiritual law in human consciousness. When you live under the jurisdiction of God, you live according to the principles revealed here. These principles are the basis for God action. Spiritual law, like all law, is designed to be acted upon. The law is not passive; it defines how individuals and institutions relate to one another, and how societies exist. These principles reveal how God functions, and how He relates to us. As we begin to understand the spiritual realm, we begin to let God function through and *as* us.

Oneness

~

Hear, O Israel, the Lord our God is one...

DEUT 6:5

One source, one substance, one life–this is the foundation of mysticism. There is not God *and* anything else. There is not God *and* man. There is not God *and* life. There is not God *and* creation. There is only God. The above quote from Deuteronomy continues: "And thou shalt love the Lord thy God with all thine heart, and with all thy soul, and with all thy might."[24] This is the first commandment Jesus gave when he said there were only two great commandments. The other was to love your neighbor as your self. If there is only one God, then there is only one Self. When you love your neighbor as your self, you see him as he truly is–an expression of God. It doesn't matter how he appears, or how he behaves. His spiritual nature is one with all spiritual creation, and he is a unique expression of God.

Oneness is the key to spiritual freedom. It is what Jesus knew. It is what Isaiah knew. It is what Moses, Shankara, Lao Tzu, and all the great mystics knew. This principle of oneness is the secret that has performed miracles, manifested abundance, and lifted man out of limited states of thinking throughout the ages. It allows those who are sufficiently attuned and have the desire to know the spiritual aspect of life to live as instruments of God and open the soul center in all they meet.

It takes practice to shift from your conditioned perspective, which is based on material information, to a spiritual perspective.

A common perception of God is that He is a mighty Judge, King of Heaven and Earth, an eternal Santa Claus who gives and withholds, blesses and curses. That concept sets up a separation between God and man. As human beings, we are not eternal, and few are kings or queens. This idea of God as a judge probably comes from mankind's own human desire for vengeance and retribution, and it motivates man to make God in his own image and likeness. Such a conditioned concept of God perpetuates the belief that man is separate and apart from God; it perpetuates a sense of duality that is the root of contention and conflict. You pray and nothing happens. You get angry that God seems to pay no attention to you. You see so much human suffering that you abandon God entirely. Yet, if you do abandon that human concept of God, you have actually taken the first step toward knowing God, "whom to know aright is life eternal."[25] If you think that God is infinite and you are finite, you preclude any experience of oneness. If you think that you are separate and abandoned, left to the whims of material belief, your life will unfold according to your beliefs.

When you realize that there is no God out there, you open yourself to the experience of mystical union, or direct communion with ultimate Reality. This spiritual union or oneness does not have the same meaning as the word "one" in common terms. It is not the opposite of many. It is the experience of the non-dual realm of Spirit. As I said earlier, there is not God and man. There is only God: one Being, one creation, one Life. Your conscious union with God is a state of oneness. In that experience your dualistic conditioning dissolves. There is no more good and evil, spiritual and human; there is only God. In this experience of deep silence, your perceptions change. You discover that God is within you and, at the same time without, comprising the totality of creation. You go beyond the conceptual world that has defined your existence until now, into the realm of spirit where you are the alpha and omega.

This is the mystery of spiritual living. You are at once the center and circumference of all being. The spiritual self within you is greater than anything in the world. Disease is not greater than this inner self. War is not greater than the spirit of God within you. Tyranny and oppression cannot limit the spirit of God within you. Your freedom in this world is not dependent upon or conditioned by any material power. In your oneness with God, you live in a state of spiritual freedom, wholeness, and fulfillment. When this is realized within, it appears in the "without," and the without is influenced by an inner joy.

The revelation of Oneness by Jewish mystics has been veiled by both the Jewish clergy and the Christian Church. Their fear has been that man would think that in his human state, he is God. But, the moment you personalize the experience of Oneness, it is gone from your experience. So, when Jesus said that he was the alpha and omega–the beginning and the end–he was speaking as the Christ, that spiritual nature resident in all mankind. When people tried to personalize the expression of God to Jesus, he said, "Why call me good?"[26] The Christ is the "I" of you, as it was the "I" of Jesus. It is your Soul. The "I" of you is the beginning and the end, the completion of the circle of eternity. The realization of this brings you into a state of oneness with all creation.

As I mentioned earlier, when I was a young man, I sailed the South Pacific in a fifty-foot ketch. The voyage became a spiritual initiation for me; and, one night I had an experience that revealed to me the nature of oneness. This experience came toward the end of our trip while sailing back to Hawaii from the Marquises Islands. During the months prior to this time, my relationship with the owner and captain of the yacht had become strained. Our perceptions of each other were rather low, and I felt quite alone and abandoned. My shipmates tried to lift my spirits, telling me that the cause of the discord was the owner's fault, but the friendship and support of others wasn't what I needed. I needed to step out of a relationship based on human cause and effect and into a deeper sense of my true self.

It happened one night near the equator. We were in the doldrums without any wind. The sails were up, but they hung limp.

The owner refused to waste precious fuel to take us to the trade winds that were a hundred miles north. So, we drifted on a flat, glassy sea.

I had the late watch and was alone on deck from midnight to the early morning. The sky was cloudless and without a moon. The stars shone so brightly that they were reflected in the water. I stood on the rail, hanging onto the shrouds, and stared down at the reflection of the heavens in the sea. Soon my thoughts turned away from my unbearable situation to the beauty at my feet–the stars shining in the sea. A statement from Mrs. Eddy came to me: "God is at once the center and circumference of being."[27] At that moment, I found myself becoming one with the sea. I almost wanted to let go of the shrouds and fall into the water, but instead the sea came up to me. All that I knew of the sea–its warmth, its saltiness, and its power–filled my awareness until there was no longer the sea and me; there was only one.

Then I was filled with the heavens. I looked up and saw the infinite stretch of the stars that a moment before were just reflections on the surface of the water. They drew me to the edge of the universe. In that moment, I knew that the earth and the heavens were within me, within my consciousness. They were as much a part of me as I was of them. There was no barrier, no separation between my environment and me. There was only one.

In that moment of oneness, I was filled with an incredible love. The loneliness left me. What did I need with man whose breath was in his nostrils? I was one with all mankind in my oneness with God. I could be alone in a desert and be connected with my fellow man. I could be adrift, alone in the middle of the Pacific Ocean, and not be separated from those who brought me peace. I was fulfilled in that moment, and I understood that everything necessary for my well being was in an experience of Oneness.

The realized consciousness of Oneness is the healing consciousness. Spiritual healing is not achieved through a human being; it is an activity of that divine Spirit within. When you realize the presence of God within yourself, you come under spiritual law, and you bring others into this universal healing consciousness. In the consciousness of Oneness there ceases to be separate individuals–one who needs something and another who gives it. Both individuals are united in the oneness of God; in that union, only the manifestation of God exists. This union is not static, though it is experienced in a state of absolute stillness and peace. Its dynamic is a love that falls on the just and the unjust. In this atmosphere judgment does not exist. You are in a non-dual state and experience God without concept or image. The result of this experience reveals the Reality of being, which appears to human sense as healing.

In the state of realized Oneness, you fulfill the commandment to make no idol or image of God. On the surface, that commandment seems to address worshipping some material form that represents divine power; but, mystically you know that any mental image or concept of God is an idol. Mystical union with God is the prayer taught by the great masters and is a state of Being beyond words, thoughts, hopes, and desires. It is a state of Oneness.

God is Reality. There is no reality separate from God. You exist within God, and God is manifest through you and as you. You can never separate yourself from God except in your own mind. When you use your mind as a conduit for Spirit, you let go of the concepts that create your earthly experience and glimpse the underlying spiritual reality of all that exists. As you see the universal foundation of life as spiritual, you realize that you exist in the realm of Spirit while seeming to live in the physical world.

This realization puts you in the position to choose. If you choose to align with Spirit, you experience Oneness and God manifests spiritually through you. To the degree that spiritual purity is established in your mind, you experience Divine Good in all its infinite variety. On the other hand, if you choose to align with the material world either through ignorance or habit, you will function according to the dictates of your concepts.

When you accept the material idea that there is a power outside of God (material cause and effect), you live in the realm of duality. In that realm you appear separate from the oneness of God and live with the idea that there is God *and* man. From a material perspective, you would reason: "I am here, you are there. Where is God?" However, the spiritual reality is: The *I* that I am *is* the Divine Self. It is not only the Self of me; it is the Self of you. It is not a personal self that I alone have. It is a universal Self. It is "*I*-myself," and also "*I*-you," devoid of human concept. When I contact this *I*, I contact not only the universal Self that I am, but I also contact *you*–not your humanhood or personality, but your Spiritual Identity.

Jesus said, "And I, if I be lifted up from the earth, will draw all men unto me."[28] There is only one Self, and that Self is expressed individually. No two individual expressions are alike, and yet spiritually, we are all one. This is not a Oneness that is the opposite of many; it is a Oneness that is an experience of the presence of God because God is One. God is non-dual. Since there is nothing other than God, God is free to manifest Itself one hundred percent *beyond* us, as well as one hundred percent *within* us.

When you experience the presence of God, there is no duality in that experience. There is no "*and*." There is just God. God cannot be held in the mind. God is not a belief, a concept, a thought, or an idea. God is an experience. When you experience the Presence of God, you experience a deep state of peace. You understand that the peace of God is omnipotence. There is nothing on earth more powerful than that Presence and atmosphere; and, when you let that experience really sink into the consciousness that you are–not your brain and not your mind–you find freedom and joy.

ONENESS IS A STATE OF BEING

Impersonalization is the Way to Move into Action

Impersonalization is the first great healing principle. It removes the personal sense of good that says, "my good is dependent on a person." It also removes the personification of evil, the belief that there is a devil or Satan causing suffering. If God is one, the universal Cause for all that exists in the universe, then the only effect or manifestation of that Cause must be spiritual and include all that God is. The material appearance of cause and effect (or action and reaction) is the belief in karma. Your realization of the oneness of God dissolves that belief. Karma is one of the most ingrained concepts held by mankind. We are always seeking a reason for what is happening to us. Is something in the past responsible for something happening now? If you believe in reincarnation, that past could include many lifetimes.

When Jesus meets a blind man–a story repeated in all the gospels–the people around Jesus ask him who "sinned" to bring about the condition. In essence, they were asking what material cause brought about the blindness. Blindness could be a metaphor for any universal limitation from which we suffer. Jesus said that no one sinned. That response immediately eliminated a material cause to the problem, and the man was healed. Then Jesus said, "...but that the works of God should be made manifest in him."[29] Some interpret this as removing the burden from the man or his parents and putting it on God. But, God is only good, thus God cannot be the cause of human suffering. With this healing, Jesus also nullified an old Hebrew law that said the sins of the father are visited on the children for generations.[30] A more mystical interpretation would be that Jesus in his Christhood, in conscious union with God, nullified the power of blindness and revealed the omnipotence of God. Other gospels tell of Jesus healing a blind man. In those gospels Jesus tells the man, who regained his sight, that his "faith has made him well," or his "faith has saved him," and that he should "tell no one of the healing." What is the point here? It demonstrates the nature of *Impersonalization.*

Jesus gave no personal cause to the problem. Neither the man or his parents sinned that he should be born blind. In the story in Mark, Jesus also took no credit for the healing, telling the man that it was his faith that made him whole. What was that faith? That God would heal him of blindness? No, it was when someone functioning under spiritual law came into his presence, that no other power could manifest but God. The healing took place because the man accepted his spiritual birthright. In that instant he was freed from material law and its limitations. By telling the man to tell no one, Jesus keeps this experience in the realm of the impersonal. There are no bragging rights. No one can say that so-and-so healed me, or that someone in his or her humanhood can be a healer. Spiritual healing takes place where there is no person to be sick and no person to heal them. All there is in spiritual healing is the nature of God realized, and in that realization only God is manifested.

A few years ago my wife Sandra and I saw how impersonalization worked in a business situation. But, before I go into the story, I want to remind you that these principles all work in concert. They are an orchestra creating spiritual vibrations in harmony with universal principles. Giving an example of how impersonalization works is like focusing on a cello and describing its importance to the orchestra.

We own a commercial building where we keep an office. One company, let's call them "XYZ Company," rented all the other offices in the building. In order for us to use our office, we had to walk through their space. This arrangement was quite harmonious until the owner of the company approached me wanting to buy the property. He was a charming man. He had a way of dealing with people that drew them into his world and got them to see things through his eyes. He had all the reasons why it would be in my best interest to sell my property to him, but I didn't want to sell. When I turned him down a third time, I sensed something changed in him.

A warehouse was connected to the office building and, at that time, a chemical company rented the warehouse. Soon after I refused to sell the property to XYZ Company, their employees began saying they were sick. They blamed their illness on the chemical company, and soon city inspectors came to scrutinize my building for zoning, fire and safety violations. In addition, XYZ Company stopped paying their rent, though they continued to occupy their offices. Then, XYZ Company sued me. I was blamed for making their employees sick while they continued to do business in their offices without paying rent. Sandra and I still worked every day in our office, breathing the same air and enduring the hostility of XYZ's employees for months while the attorneys tried to resolve the problem.

Every day before going to work, Sandra and I would clear our mind of any judgment or concept we held about XYZ Company, its president and its employees. We meditated until we felt the silence of "My peace," and then began our day. Often, that peace was shattered as we walked to our office, not by any overt action, but by the hostile atmosphere. From my perspective, it was an injustice and I reacted to it. I was angry that we had to spend time and money to defend ourselves from false accusations. But slowly, I would regain my peace. I would consciously remove any person from the situation, placing what was happening in the context of universal belief that empowers both good and evil. If God is the only power and God is One, then any appearance of a power coming from this world cannot exist. To maintain my oneness with God, I could not attach any power to man. Whatever the appearance–a man, my neighbors, the people occupying my building–behind that appearance is God appearing as the one Self, infinitely manifested. The I of me *is* the I of you, and that is universal.

The moment I realized the spiritual oneness with those I had to meet, I could see through the personality, through the conditioned person, to where the Christ dwelled. The change happened one day as I was going through the XYZ space to our office. I ran into the president, who was the seeming cause to all these problems, and I had no reaction to him. I faced my "enemy," and there was neither attraction nor fear. I didn't want to see this man suffer the consequences of his actions, nor did I seek anything from him, like an apology or some acknowledgement of his part in the situation. No longer was there power in the appearance. I saw through the appearance to the Christ, and all there was was love. I understood how Jesus could say, "Love your enemies." We did our work, and at the end of the day Sandra and I left knowing we were no longer attached to this drama.

That night Sandra and I celebrated. We no longer dreaded going to work. It didn't matter who was in the office; our peace and our joy could not be touched by the activities of this world. When we arrived at our building the next day, XYZ Company had moved out. Everything was gone–the furniture, files, plants, and all of their art and awards. Within a week the lawsuit was dropped and the attorneys settled without going to court.

Nowness

~

Now are we the children of God.

I JOHN 3:2

God does not function in the past or the future. Being eternal, God is beyond time and is present in every moment. God can only be experienced in the *now*. An experience of *now* is an experience of eternity because in that moment of God realization, you are one with God and all that God is. This comes as an experience of Peace. "My Peace" opens your understanding, and momentarily you feel the secrets of the universe revealed. If you look back on a God experience, you are already out of the *now*. You might find that it lasted only an instant, or you could have been in that Peace for minutes. The material relationship of time is unimportant. What feeds your soul is your acknowledgement of the Presence every moment you are aware of it. The more you live in the *now* of God, the more you live under spiritual law.

The *now* principle is the greatest healing tool. It brings the spiritual realm into your experience and, with it, spiritual law. Spiritual law does not function in the material world. It does not compete with physical law. Spiritual law exists in My Kingdom, which is the only reality there is. And, in your moments of spiritual awareness, you are in this reality under God's law. In these moments, everything in your life comes under Divine jurisdiction. This is the meaning of the following phrases: "A mind stayed on God is a law of harmony unto your being"; "Thou will keep him in perfect peace whose mind is stayed on Thee"; and, "The mind controlled by spirit is life and peace." Alignment with spiritual law only takes place in the moment when you turn within and direct your attention to the spiritual source from which all good flows. All dualistic, conflicting thought leaves your awareness, and you experience the joy of the spiritual kingdom in the *now*.

When you use your mind in your normal human thought processes, you are locked into time and space. You relate to the material world and process the events you experience according to your beliefs about time and space. That is the nature of this world. When you experience the presence of God in the *now*, your mind is used in a different way. It becomes an instrument of God and functions to bring the spiritual dimension into your life.

When you realize that your mind is a tool, you gain a degree of control over it. You no longer react from a strictly personal basis to the thoughts that come into your awareness. Instead, you watch that mental activity with detachment, knowing that the basic thoughts coming to you are impersonal and universal. What makes those thoughts "yours" is identifying with them, and that takes you out of the *now* and into the past or future. All thoughts exist in the dimension of time. When you go into meditation, you leave the world of thought and time and enter a state of *now*-ness. There you can experience all that God is.

Having a mind attuned to God begins to shift your perspective. What you see in the *now* alters what you see through your senses. For example, suppose you have a problem and decide to solve it spiritually. You take the metaphysical steps to mentally remove any sense of power from the problem and then, when your mind is free from wanting to solve the problem on the level of the problem, you begin to contemplate the nature of God. Soon, thoughts stop and you experience the Presence in the *now*. If a spiritual connection was made in the *now,* when your thoughts resume, you will look at the problem and see it differently. If it was a health problem, the fear is gone and a healing occurs. Even if the appearances haven't disappeared, you know a transformation took place within, in the *now*, and without judgment, you can watch the outer change take place. If the problem was of a different nature, the solution comes to you from that moment of spiritual connectedness and will manifest in your awareness.

If fear motivates your spiritual progress, you are still functioning from orthodox conditioning. Both mainstream religions and some metaphysical movements have the idea that if you aren't praying and doing some kind of protective work, you will suffer some sort of evil. This idea is erroneous. Certainly, if you accept the evils of this world as power, you probably will suffer from that belief. But, when you remember the principle of oneness and enter that consciousness in the *now*, the fearful appearances, thoughts, or ideas lose their sense of power. Your protection in this world does not come from trying to protect yourself from evil; rather, it is in your conscious realization of the presence of God. And, that realization can only take place in the *now*.

Fear comes into your experience through judgment. If you judge the conceptual world as evil, you fear it. If you accept "this world" as the opposite of My Kingdom, you create a sense of separation between yourself and the spirit within. My Kingdom is not a place. My Kingdom is a state of oneness. Therefore, it has no opposite and exists in the eternity of *now*. It is an error to accept suffering as a condition related to your lack of spiritual awareness. That way of thinking misses the point. It still perceives life through dualistic conditioning. Regardless of the appearance, God is here and now. Withdraw the judgment; stop asking yourself why this is happening to you; and, enter the *now*. There you will find freedom and joy.

Remember, there is not God *and* man. The mental attitude of separation, which time and space define, gives power to the material realm. What removes that power is the knowledge that at any moment you can be in My Kingdom. That knowledge gives you the freedom to be in the world and participate in your business, your profession, or even in politics with the perspective that in your moments of spiritual awareness, the *I* of you brings the entire spiritual dimension into your experience. There is no process because it only happens in the *now*.

Meditation is the way to establish your awareness of the spiritual dimension. Mystics have used various forms of meditation over the centuries to experience the consciousness of oneness. Some have gone into trances and are consciously removed from this world. Their bodies are left in time and space in some form of suspended animation, awaiting their return. Other mystical traditions use dance to step out of the thinking process and achieve a state of bliss. A more contemporary way of meditation is to become aware of your thought process and observe it without judgment.

As you dispassionately watch your thoughts, you discover that without your attention to them, they diminish, and soon your mind is quiet. You will notice that there are spaces between your thoughts, and those spaces are still and silent. This is universal. No matter how much your mind races, there are always spaces between the thoughts. You become receptive to spiritual impartations in the stillness between thoughts. It is in an atmosphere of peace that you experience the divine Presence, which is universal and always with you. As you become more and more familiar with this state of consciousness, you realize that this world is not a separate realm. It is My Kingdom seen through a human perspective.

Actually, there is only one Kingdom. You might be immersed in the drama of human experience, but spiritual Reality always is here and *now*. What appears to be an either/or situation–"this world" or "My Kingdom"–is really an illusion, just "smoke and mirrors" tricking you into believing that you are cut off from your Source and must depend on some process to unite with Spirit. This illusion is like the Zen koan that asks the student how to get the goose out of the bottle. The ego attempts to answer the unanswerable, and tricks you into focusing on the outer so that you can't experience the inner. To try to spiritualize this world is impossible. From the spiritual perspective of *now*, you have never left the Kingdom no matter how immersed you are in material sense.

As a human being, your life is measured in time. You observe all the stages of life, from infancy to old age, and accept that this is what life is. The past can be pleasant or painful. It can cause you to fear, or it can bring happy memories. In fact, both fear and desire are derivatives of time. Both require memory and/or mental projections to have power. Those with some developed spiritual sense find that in times of crises, the immediacy of Spirit, the *nowness* of your spiritual Self, comes forward and fear is instantaneously replaced by peace. You can't plan for this to happen, or anticipate it. There is no process to it. However, you can develop your ability to be in the *now* by meditating. The more you experience mystical union, consciously realizing the presence of God in that inner silence, the more you step out of the conditioned realm of time. Eventually you will discover that no matter what you are doing, if you have developed that "listening ear," you will be living in the *now*.

Everything seems to progress from birth to death. We even describe the stars and galaxies in terms of birth and death. All physical observation testifies to this pattern. To material sense, time is the agent of death. Once again you are confronted with a paradox: If God is your being, and God is eternal, why is there death? And, once again, you come back to the mystical revelation that "My kingdom is not of this world." With what do you identify? Can you choose between the flesh and the spirit? There is a way, but it requires a shift in perception.

Mystical living is being in the world but not of it. It is seeing all of creation, not just the dualistic half that came after the introduction of time. All physical form comes and goes. When you identify with your physicality, you align yourself with material perception. If you look at God and the spiritual realm from this state, you have a sense of separation–the destructive concept that denies you your spiritual birthright. The way back to union is in the *now* moment. What happens when you become still and divorce yourself from ego, personality, and physicality? A void is created in your mentality and Spirit fills it. Concepts, which exist in time, disappear; judgments, which form over time, disappear; fear leaves. And, so does hope, for hope depends on the future for its existence. In the *now*, what is left for you to identify with? Nothing. And, therein is the mystical experience.

In Buddhism, the experience of nothingness is considered the highest point of illumination. It is Nirvana. In this state of consciousness, you are one with all spiritual form and idea, yet you are detached from all sense of material expression. You are one with spiritual law, and any material situation cannot exist because it is not a manifestation of God. In this *nowness*, as an individual, you are not projecting any personal concept to be manifested; you are a pure transparency for spiritual expression. This is a state of non-judgment, where spiritual reality is expressed in all of its purity. This is where healings take place–in the *now*.

Years ago, before the Santa Monica freeway was built, Virginia Stephenson[31] was teaching at the Los Angeles Infinite Way Center, and had to travel from the beach to the mid-town center. It was normally a forty-minute drive, though you might make it in thirty-five if you hit green lights all the way. One day, circumstances conspired to delay Virginia so that she had only ten minutes to make the trip. Instead of worrying about keeping the students waiting for so long, she tried an experiment. While driving normally, she kept herself in the *now*. Anytime a thought would enter that testified to her being late, she let it go without judgment. She didn't resist it. She didn't fight it or deny it. She just kept herself in the *now*. When she stopped at a red light, it was in the *now*. When the traffic slowed, it was still in the *now*. When she arrived at the study center, she was five minutes early! Many students could not accept what had happened because time was too much of a reality to them. They thought that surely her clocks were off. But I witnessed this. I remembered when she left!

In Truth, all is Consciousness, and Consciousness manifests Its creation in the *now*. If you are totally present, and totally still, you are like the point at which a line begins. If you stay on that point, you become the center of all that happens. You don't travel on that line out to where you think the action is; you stay on that point and *become* the action. That point is holy ground. It is not localized in matter, but exists in the *now*. Every moment that you stop and become centered, you enter a state that is beyond material measurement. Look inward into infinity and discover how universal you are. You no longer occupy space, but you *are* the inner source *and* the outer manifestation of God in action. God becomes your only definition. You live by spiritual law, and God not only manifests Itself as you, It is the world in which you live.

LIVING IN THE NOW

Bring Now-ness into Action

To be free of the restraints of the material world, you cannot judge your life or the condition of the world by how things appear. You have been conditioned your whole life to name and label your world, identifying what will help you, as well as what will harm you. This process, which is innate to the human being, creates lives and realities based on material belief. You judge from the level of appearance how something will benefit you, or hurt you, on a personal level. Material appearances seldom reveal the underlying spiritual reality. To identify with an appearance, whether it is how you see something outside yourself, or whether it is how you see yourself personally, is to identify with a concept rather than with spiritual reality. To judge "righteous judgment," you must take yourself out of the material realm of cause and effect, and bring yourself under spiritual law. This is the essence of *right identification,* a basic healing principle.

Right identification depends upon your knowing what constitutes spiritual reality regardless of the material appearance. For most people, their sense of judgment is so ingrained that they often make judgments that align them with material cause and effect without realizing it. It is much easier to accept, at face value, what your senses tell you, than it is to take a moment to determine the origin of what it is you are experiencing. In that moment, as you practice the now-ness of God, you shift your identification from the material to the spiritual. This has nothing to do with what is taking place outside of your own mentality. You are not trying to change an appearance. You are not trying to impose God on the appearance. All you are doing is recognizing where you stand at that moment in relationship to Spirit. If there is a spiritual component to what you witness, and you recognize it, you bring that spiritual truth into manifestation. If there is nothing but material concept there, you can drop it. You have made no judgment, thus you have not entered into the material concept, or picked up the sword to fight it. You have kept your being in God and His law, and in that consciousness, material appearances have no power.

Here is a healing principle. With spiritual realization (the realization that all is in Consciousness) natural disasters and other forms of disharmony dissolve. They have no material law to support them when observed from this state of spiritual awareness. Destructive power is no part of God. From the non-dual perspective of illumined consciousness, the event "out there" has no essence, no substance. As the Buddha revealed, any material concept that presents itself to you as power can exist only if it is one with God; only if it exists beyond time and space. The appearances of disease, suffering, poverty, and despair disappear in the presence of an individual with the realized consciousness of spiritual oneness. The same is true of the appearances of pleasure, wealth, and personal power. They have no residence in spiritual consciousness in their conceptual form. It is only when you withdraw all judgment from good that you experience an abundance of Grace.

You can individually practice the principles of non-judgment and right identification when you watch the news or read the newspaper. If you consciously withdraw power from the events on the world stage, and at the same time recognize any spiritual underpinnings when they appear, you fulfill the important commandment to love one another. You nullify the effect that material appearances have on you, and through the principle of oneness, you free those in your consciousness from the limitations suggested by the appearances. If there are enough of us doing this around the world, a dramatic spiritual alignment takes place. The power of *now* acts in this collective spiritual recognition, and touches all who are awake to the spiritual realm.

Another way of practicing the *now* is being mindful of what you do. If you are doing boring chores, and your mind wanders into the past or the future, you cut yourself off from the awareness of the presence of God. You are not in the *now* where God is. The Buddha taught a village woman how to be in the present by being aware of how she drew water from a well. He taught her to be aware of the precise movement of her hands and arms as she pulled up the bucket of water, and not to let her mind wander because the task was mundane. He taught her not to project what would happen next, where the water was to go, or how it was to be used. By practicing this exercise, the woman could remain in the *now* and feel the presence of God with her no matter what she was doing.

Many might not realize that the principle of "judge not after appearances" is part of the Sermon on the Mount. That sermon is the essence of the Christ teaching, and it takes a degree of spiritual discernment to grasp what Jesus was saying. This principle did not originate with Jesus; he learned it from Isaiah. So, this principle has a long history in mystical thought, and it is very practical.

We had a business situation once in which we would have been in the right to bring a lawsuit. We were working with a man, an architect, who happened to be religious, and he was helping us with the situation. He knew that we had the money to bring the suit. He couldn't understand why we didn't go to court. My mother, Virginia, brought up what Jesus said about not resisting evil, and not judging someone good or evil. The architect's answer was that those laws didn't apply to everyday life; that nobody could live like that. Even if a materialist is religious, it is almost impossible for him to not judge. His human life must be protected at all costs; good must be defended and justice served. But, material justice based on reward and punishment is not what the Christ taught. He taught forgiveness, which seems difficult to practice in a society like ours that is built on judgment. To withdraw judgment would seem to indicate that one would withdraw from society. But, the Master concluded his instruction to "judge not after appearances" with "judge righteous judgment." Righteous judgment is the ability to see through the appearance and discern its origin. It is the ability to identify with Spirit, and not to fear what this world throws at us. It is the Buddha, under the Bodhi tree, immoveable in his spiritual integrity and unconcerned with the forces of good or evil.

The question of whether evil exists is always with us. One year, even the presidential candidates were asked whether evil exists. Judging after appearances, evil is a powerful force in the world. If there is an omnipotent God, then He either condones evil by allowing it to exist; or He is the cause of evil; or He is, in fact, impotent and, therefore, irrelevant to our human existence. The presidential candidates agreed that evil existed, but they had different ways to handle it. One candidate vowed to fight it and defeat it. The other candidate, Barack Obama, thought it needed to be confronted, but with humility. He said, "Only God can defeat evil, and our good intentions do not mean that we are always doing good." When you identify with Spirit, instead of having the reactionary response of the materialist, you find another way of looking at evil.

Recently, a story circulated that addressed the question of whether evil exists. In the story, a professor postulates that since God created everything, He must have created evil, and that, therefore, God must be evil. Most of the students couldn't argue the logic of that statement–except one. He stood and asked the professor if cold existed. The professor became trapped in his own logic. Not knowing the scientific definition of "cold," he had to agree that it did. Cold is defined as the absence of heat. It does not exist in and of itself. The student then asked the professor if darkness existed. Again, the answer was that darkness does not exist; darkness is only the absence of light. Then, he asked the professor if evil existed, and the professor, following this line of thinking, had to agree that it did not. Evil is just the absence of God.[32]

Spiritually, we know that there cannot be the absence of God. Therefore, when you identify with God, you identify with all good, peace, harmony, and perfection. If you identify with material sense, which is a product of mass human judgment, you experience both good *and* evil. In this world, you may not be able to live completely without evil touching your life, but when you identify with Spirit, you deny evil its sense of power and bring yourself under spiritual law.

Isaiah describes life lived from the perspective of Spirit. To paraphrase Isaiah, when the spirit of the Lord rests upon him; the spirit of wisdom and understanding; the spirit of counsel and might; the spirit of knowledge and fear of the Lord; he shall be quick to understand the Lord, and he will not judge after the sight of his eyes or criticize after the hearing of his ears. With righteousness shall he judge the poor, and admonish with equity the meek of the earth, and he shall smite the earth with the rod of his mouth, and with the breath of his lips shall he slay the wicked.[33]

In the mystical language of the Bible, this is not the wrath and destruction of a vengeful God. It describes the character necessary to be in the world but not of it. First of all, to "fear" the Lord means to be in awe of Him, and respect *Him*. When you realize that the Lord is the *"I"* within you, this makes sense. When you know that to experience your spiritual nature, your ego nature needs to be absent, it makes sense. You come to realize that to experience omniscience, omnipresence and omnipotence, you cannot judge humanly. You have to shift into living from your spiritual awareness. When that takes place, you see the foibles of human nature with compassion and understanding, and you are not tempted to give them any power. You speak the truth, and error cannot exist. The wicked, that personalized sense of life that identifies with matter, is destroyed by the word of God, "the breath of His lips." Life is not destroyed. The individual is not destroyed. The material concept that gives power to this world and appears as evil, flees from your experience when you let go of that level of life. Paul was more blunt. He said we must "die daily" in order to experience the Christ.

What is the result of living from this premise? According to Isaiah, "The wolf shall dwell with the lamb and the child will play on the hole of the asp; nations will beat their swords into plowshares and their spears into pruning hooks and no longer will they train for war; there shall be no pain or destruction in all My holy mountain; for the earth shall be full of the knowledge of the Lord as the waters cover the sea."[34] This is not a prophecy, but a description of living in peace and safety when we live in the *now*.

Completeness

~

In Him dwells all the fullness of the Godhead bodily.
And ye are complete in Him…

COLOSSIANS 2:9-10

If we look at life from a scientific perspective, especially one that includes the realm of quantum mechanics, we must conclude that everything that has ever, or will ever exist, exists now. It is called by various names, such as the quantum soup, unmanifested field of intelligence, or undifferentiated being. Following the quantum model, it takes an observer to manifest matter, that is, to change the wave energy into a particle. Who is that observer on the universal scale? If we accept the "big bang" theory, what existed in the beginning still exists today. In whatever environment the "big bang" took place, that environment–Consciousness–still exists today. Has anything been added to the universe? Has anything been taken away? The forms might change, as in the coming and going of stars, but the substance is still here in its completeness as it was in the beginning. The Consciousness that witnessed the formation of the universe is the form itself. This has been termed the "Self aware universe."

Let's move into the mystical and bring in the principle of oneness. The Consciousness that brought forth creation, that witnessed the "big bang" if you will, is the substance and form of all that exists. In essence, the universe and all that is in it is spiritual. The observed and the observer are one. That means that you and I are one and inseparable from the whole of creation. We are of one substance, manifesting according to universal law. Infinite Consciousness expresses Itself as individual being, and that expression lives in perfect harmony serving the One. Each aspect of creation plays an integral part in expressing the whole. Whether it moves through the universe as a planet or a star, or if it takes the form of sentient beings, the life of every part of the whole is governed by the power, intelligence, and love of Infinite Consciousness. No part of creation is unmanifested. As we accept this description of existence, we become receptive to spiritual law.

But, if we look at the universe as material (the result of an event in time) and speculate that there is a spiritual realm somewhere out there (separate from the rest of creation) we do what human beings have done since the beginning. We conceive a dual creation–one material and the other spiritual. If we have God "out there" responsible for everything, and then separate ourselves not only from Him but from the substance of creation, we have made a mistake. If we think we are spiritual, but living in a material world, we cut ourselves off from our Source. Instead of heaven and earth, we have spiritual creation and material sense. This is not correct. God is the substance of all that exists. So, the question is, does that make God part of evil, suffering, disease and death? The answer is no, and this is why.

The way quantum theory applies to our physical existence is in the idea that what appears in our experience is there because of what we hold in consciousness, that is, what we take from the quantum soup. The quantum soup, or the collective mind, is not Infinite Consciousness. It is the realm of human experience and consists of the judgments collected throughout the ages. What comes into manifestation from this realm is the result of all the beliefs, ideas, and concepts resident in the conditioned mind. As universal human consciousness grows in spiritual awareness, many of the beliefs and concepts once believed to be true fall out of the soup. Many are replaced with new concepts. Concepts are nothing more than human judgments accepted on a mass scale. So, whatever thought you accept as true, whether it is based on fact or belief, will manifest itself in your experience as long as you live from a materialistic perception. When there is no awareness of the oneness and *nowness* of God, you draw from this quantum soup the building blocks of your human life according to your fears and desires. This principle applies to any situation.

For example, it could apply to your body. You feel a pain in your chest and think "heart attack." That thought instigates fear, and the fear produces a reaction that makes your heart race, and you panic. You remain in this state until someone in authority either confirms or denies your supposition. If it wasn't a heart attack, you experienced something manifested by your belief. If, on the other hand, you were aware of the presence of God, that activity in consciousness would bring peace. And, from that peace would come the correct action.

It could also apply to your feelings and emotions. An insult can generate hatred towards an individual and your judgment of that individual can create an enemy. Thinking that the behavior of certain groups of people is socially unacceptable, especially if it is a different ethnic group from yours, can create prejudice and perpetuate stereotypes. What is prejudice but pre-judging according to your belief of right and wrong? These thoughts can manifest by drawing into your experience those who upset you. When you let go of the judgment, that "draw" is gone.

This quantum idea (sometimes called the law of attraction) affects how we react to the physical world, how we see ourselves in society, and how we relate to others. All of the good and evil we experience is the result of human conditioning, and this conditioning is universal. To the degree that we identify with and personalize this universal conditioning, we give it power and bring that sense of power into our experience. As we desire the "good" things in life–family, friends, home, meaningful work, and a healthy body–we manifest that personal sense of good. Conversely, as we fear suffering, conflict, disease, and death, those concepts also manifest as part of our experience. There seems to be a constant struggle between these elements of good and evil, and the universal prayer is for God to save us. But, there is no God in that sense of life. There is no God in any material concept or human judgment. There is nothing God can add to your life because all that God is, is happening now. The only way to experience spiritual freedom is to recognize that truth. Recognize that God knows nothing of human life. God knows only Itself, and you know that Self when you step out of the conceptual world, out of that quantum soup, and into the reality of spiritual creation.

When you hear a teacher talk about the unseen reality, what does that mean? It seems like there are two realities–a spiritual reality *and* a relative material reality. But, there are not. The relative material reality is a product of our conditioning. We've grown up with it. We taste it, touch it, see it, smell it, and hear it. We understand it to a degree, and we continually judge it either good or evil. At the same time, in the *now*, you exist spiritually. You have a relationship with all of creation. That relationship is complete, meaning that there is nothing that can be added to your life and nothing that can be taken away. This is spiritual Reality, and it is known through your soul. You experience it when you are in great joy, and suddenly feel connected to the whole earth but you can't explain why. Or, you suddenly feel a thrill–in Hawaii they call it "chicken skin"–when something is said, and intuitively you know it is true. Or, you witness something incredibly beautiful and you know you are part of that beauty. Music can bring about this experience when some melody touches your soul, takes you out of your thought process, and for a moment you experience bliss. These experiences indicate a truth beyond all concepts, and if we acknowledge them, we open ourselves to the spirit within. We discover a realm that is here and now. This realm is not separate from the world we live in, but rather it functions under a different law, a different jurisdiction than the one construed by our concepts and beliefs. This realm is the Infinite Invisible.

"God is the form, the substance and the law of *all* creation, including our body (and the world around us). Our body is not material, nor is the food we eat material. They are spiritual. *It is only our concept of creation that is material.*"[35] In the moment that you experience the oneness of mystical union, you remove from your consciousness all human belief, just as new water poured into a pitcher forces out the old. Material belief cannot coexist with spiritual reality because material belief has no substance or causal power to it. The manifestations of material belief only appear as real to the person who gives them reality by accepting them, or they appear universally real through mass acceptance. We build this reality by codifying, judging, naming, and identifying material phenomena, and ordering it in our consciousness. This human order has created a conceptual world that may, or may not, be a manifestation of spiritual reality. You can determine this by applying spiritual principles to the appearance world. Spirit is complete and wholly good. There is not a destructive element in God. If something you experience appears destructive, you remove any power it has over you in your realization of the presence of God. You remove any sense of lack or sorrow in your experience by realizing your completeness in God. If you witness acts of unconditioned love, acts of forgiveness and compassion, you take them out of the personal by recognizing those acts are God working through individual consciousness.

An individual who has some degree of illumination will experience the "Word made flesh" because the spiritually-attuned individual is complete and already has the wholeness, freedom, abundance and joy that exist in God. In fact, in your realization of God, you *are* all of that. Why, then, would you want to change the human picture when in the *now* moment you can experience and manifest all the good that God is? Why settle for patching up material concepts when you can demonstrate spiritual reality? Our oneness with God, which is our essential state of being, reveals to us the completeness of our lives. Our conscious awareness of the *I* of our being removes every material limitation, and restores our spiritual birthright. If our material belief has manifested as a lack of some kind, once we have the conscious awareness of the *I* of our being, the appropriate supply will manifest. The concept that this world is material is false. When the Word is made flesh and dwells amongst us, we live in this world but we are not of it.

So, where actually do you live? Do you live in your mind and thoughts? Do you live confined by time and space? Or, do you live in Consciousness? If you live in Consciousness, then you are complete. Nothing can be added to Consciousness, just as nothing can be added to or removed from God. When God "gives," nothing is really added, or taken away, because that gift exists in eternity. It is only from a material perception that it appears as if something has been added to you. In reality, that which seems to have been added is actually your expanding spiritual awareness of what already exists, unfolding in your consciousness. When you give from your soul, nothing is taken away. In fact, giving on the soul level opens your perception to the wholeness of God, because God functions in this attitude of selfless being. That selfless state opens the doors of abundance in your life.

However, motive is important. You experience Oneness *only* when you are free of the thought process and your mind becomes an avenue of spiritual awareness. To be in the *now*, you must be free of thoughts about the past and future, and be attentive to the moment. To experience the wholeness of God–"wholeness" being a synonym for completeness–you can have no material agenda; that is, you must be sure that you do not go to that inner place for anything material, such as healing, supply, or personal recognition.

All that is, exists in Consciousness. This fact is impossible to grasp with our limited human faculties. Even looking at the stars on a cloudless night, with all the wonder and expansiveness of that experience, can't come close to the realization of "I have." *If I have Consciousness, then I have all.* How do we know this? In our moments of total stillness, where time ceases and we enter the void of *no-thing-ness*, there is a Presence that fills us with peace. This Presence cannot be defined in words, but when you experience

It, you know It, and become one with It. In this non-dual nature, you know the only source, cause, and substance of Life. Here there is only one. Shift out of concept into Consciousness, and be complete. All the great mystical masters have taught this principle. Once you get it, once you see that in this state of consciousness is all that exists, you stop looking for good from a material perspective. This takes practice. If you feel the Presence and nothing changes in your life, look deeply at your motives. One of the great paradoxes of mystical living is that to gain your life, you must lose your life. Are you willing to take that step? If you are, and you realize that the silence that comes with the Presence is omnipotent, you will see harmony, abundance, and the fullness of joy in your life. But, you have to trust in that Presence, in the unseen reality *here and now.*

Everything you experience in this world is filtered through your human sense of consciousness. The infinite nature of creation is limited by the concepts you put upon it. As humans, we observe though our senses, but our sensory perceptions are limited. Our ears hear only part of the spectrum of sound that surrounds us. Our eyes see only the light existing between infrared and ultraviolet. Anything outside those parameters is invisible. Judgment further limits what you experience. You might intuitively know that there is more to life than you are currently experiencing, but to grasp what that is takes the discipline to go within and commune with the Source of all good, the Source of life, itself. This is the only way to experience the wholeness of spirit.

Again, the secret is in the unseen reality. The only way to know the activity of truth in your consciousness is by your spiritual fruitage. We are taught to look at teachers, gurus, or practitioners by their fruits and judge accordingly. What constitutes spiritual fruitage? Is it a healthy body? Is it a fat wallet? Or, is it the degree of spiritual freedom the teacher exhibits? That is the key. Spiritual freedom is experienced in the context of a finished kingdom. It is defined by the attitude of "having," and expressed by your *being* that which is "the need" of the moment. In your oneness with the infinite, you are that form and idea, complete in this moment, to fulfill your spiritual destiny. This is true prayer. Mystically, prayer has been defined as an "altitude" and an "attitude." The altitude is in your realization of God; the attitude is your conviction that all already *is*. Then, you become a witness and watch Spirit unfold in your life.

We know from metaphysics that the mind is a powerful tool. It fashions our persona in this world and defines our life experience. Collectively, the human mind forms our world through judgment, belief, observation, and reason. Judgment begins in the earliest moments of life. Our own experience, coupled with our parents' judgments, fill our mind with concepts that appear as who we think we are and define the environment in which we live. Unless those who love us hold us in spiritual consciousness, we soon lose our awareness of the spiritual aspect of life. Being mindful of how our mind is conditioned helps us move towards the middle path, where the light of truth illumines our way. We are never separated from our spiritual wholeness, but we can be buried by concepts.

This is reminiscent of a story told by Jerry Jampolsky at one of his talks. A couple had a new born baby and a four-year-old child. When the infant was alone in its crib, the parents kept a monitor in the room so they could hear if anything was amiss. One evening the four-year-old asked if he could visit his new little sister alone. At first, the parents resisted the idea. They weren't sure what the older child was up to, or what his motive was. Finally, they agreed and when the older child went into the baby's bedroom, they turned up the monitor. There was silence for a while, and then the older child whispered to his baby sister, "Remind me what God is like. I'm beginning to forget."

Where did all this human knowledge come from in the first place? And, how do we relate to it as students of mysticism? All human knowledge began with judgment. In the legends of the Old Testament, it began with Adam. He was commanded by God to name everything in the Garden of Eden. We are still naming and labeling our world down to the tiniest quark. Then, to become like "gods," Adam and Eve ate of the fruit of the Tree of the Knowledge of Good and Evil. So, humankind began judging. Around the world, naming and judging the things and experiences encountered in life created material concepts of reality. All of this racial history and knowledge cannot be stored in the brain. As I said earlier, our brains have a limited capacity to process what is necessary to function in today's life, so there is a universal "outer mind" that holds human conditioning. This outer mind goes by many different names. Paul called it "the carnal mind"; Mary Baker Eddy termed it "mortal mind"; and, Joel Goldsmith referred to it as "conditioned mind." No matter what you call it, there is nothing spiritual about it. Mystical students know that there is another dimension to mind, one that gives access to Spirit. That mind comes to us when we go beyond the realm of words, thoughts, and concepts.

Reasoning from erroneous beliefs has limited mankind throughout history. Those who understand the working of this outer mind, or conditioned mind, discover how it can be used to influence and control. But, the sense of power they discover is only the appearance of power. In the presence of someone attuned to Spirit through the unconditioned mind, mental power is nothing more than smoke and mirrors. If you are hypnotized and accept material beliefs as power, then you experience that power. That experience can be positive or negative. But, either way, it does not touch your soul. Your soul is always complete and free. Unless you are alert to this mental realm, and can commune with the spirit within, you become another mortal adding to the picture of material concepts.

I saw a graphic example of this type of reasoning forty-some years ago on my first trip to Europe. I took a tour of East Berlin during the height of the Cold War, when East Berlin was under communist control. The clash of concepts was both startling and funny. The propaganda that insisted the communist system was better than the capitalist system was childish, especially when there was a thriving Western city, West Berlin, in their midst. But, it showed me how the belief in a concept could hypnotize a people into thinking drab was colorful, tyranny gave greater freedom, and state-generated wealth brought greater abundance. The idea that there are limited resources that have to be divided is the opposite of the realization of spiritual completeness.

We crossed into East Berlin at Checkpoint Charlie. We were held in "no-man's land" for almost an hour while our passports were taken. We were asked to show the authorities how much money we were carrying. Once it was determined how much money everyone had, we were forced to change a certain percentage into East German Marks. It was the beginning of the hypocrisy that comes with a state of consciousness that gives great authority to an ideology. It doesn't matter if the ideology is religious or secular, if it gives power to a special group of people; it has no link to spiritual reality. Spirit doesn't need any person or organization to bring forth abundance. All It needs is the soul of man.

Once we entered East Berlin, martial music filled our bus and our guide boasted of the greatness of their system. The music was supposed to emotionally prepare us for the glories we were about to see, and our tour guide's speech corrected any "misconceptions" we might have towards their system. We drove down a wide boulevard lined with high-rise apartment buildings that had stores on the ground floor. Consumer goods–refrigerators, appliances, and furniture–made everything look as successful as the West; but, they were all props. There was nothing behind the display windows but vacant space! It made me think of the lengths people will go to in order to appear prosperous. To get out of this picture, I just took the bus back to the West. But, to free ourselves from the appearance of lack in this world requires a change of perspective from the visible to the invisible.

The application of completeness in our experience is through the idea that "I have." "Thou art ever with me and all that *I have* is thine."[36] "*I have* meat you know not of."[37]

Nowhere in mystical living is there the concept of "I need," or "I want." The bridge to experiencing the abundance of the *inner* in the *outer* is consciousness. There is a sense that consciousness evolves, but that is from the material perspective. Our individual awareness of consciousness grows as we become more proficient in reaching our inner Source. Consciousness, itself, is always complete. When we experience oneness, a complete unity with Consciousness, it is an experience of a non-dual moment and always takes expression. There is no unmanifested God or good. That we don't perceive it doesn't mean it doesn't exist. Yet, don't think of this realm as a cosmic soup filled with infinite possibilities waiting for recognition. Creation is already recognized by the Creator, Itself; and, to the degree that we enter the consciousness of the Creator, we experience all that God is *and* Its manifestation.

If we feel that we are lacking, or that we are unfulfilled, we have not seen through the appearance of God "*and*." We are hypnotized by the propaganda that there is something out there in the world that will meet all our needs. Everything we experience in this world is filtered through our conditioned sense of mind, except when we are in a state of oneness and our mind is a transparency for divine Consciousness. In that elevated consciousness, the material manifestations conform to their spiritual prototypes, free of human concept. Instead of seeing the façade of a spiritual manifestation, we see the substance and reality of it. That experience brings us back into our Soul center, and we realize again that our oneness with God makes us one with all creation. Any feeling of lack or discontent vanishes, and in the bliss of oneness everything necessary for us to function as instruments of God appears.

When the elements of your life come from your conditioned sense of the world, from that outer mind of human belief, those elements carry with them all the rules of behavior your belief system imposes on them. A person might be helpful or mean, loving or hateful, depending on your conditioning as to how he looks and what he does. Physical sensations are the most obvious example of how your conditioning works. How much fear does the sensation bring? How much do you desire the sensation? These questions reveal how linked you are to the conditioned world. The more you react, the more you are coupled to the concept. It doesn't matter if the reaction is positive or negative. Your relationships carry the same elements, as well. What is the level of desire, fear, or repulsion there? The more dramatic your life, the more desire and loss affect your equilibrium. To be peaceful, where you can experience the wholeness of spiritual being, requires detaching yourself from your concepts of good and evil. Those concepts will be replaced by spiritual reality through an activity of your soul. Your conditioned concepts create your experience, but when you go beyond them and see with your spiritual faculties, you behold the Christ, that part of you created in the image and likeness of God. In that state, you are free of limited human conditioning. You are not hypnotized by the collective human belief in dualism. And, you experience the spiritual while still in the world.

Completeness is the "don't worry, be happy" principle. How liberating for us to know we are already complete and whole. Suddenly, there is no more struggle or quest. Like the Knights of the Holy Grail, the moment we give up the search for fulfillment in the outer world, our inner world opens to us. In the Book of Luke, Jesus gives us the attitude to live in this consciousness; "...take no thought about your life," or as some versions say, "Don't be anxious, don't worry about what you will eat, what you will put on." Life is more than food, and the body *is more* than clothing. Consider the ravens, for they neither sow nor reap, which have neither storehouse nor barn; and God feeds them. Of how much more value are you than the birds? And which of you by worrying can add one cubit to his stature? If you then are not able to do the least, why are you anxious for the rest? Consider the lilies, how they grow: they neither toil nor spin; and yet I say to you, even Solomon in all his glory was not arrayed like one of these. If then God so clothes the grass, which today is in the field and tomorrow is thrown into the oven, how much more *will He clothe* you, O *you* of little faith? But seek the kingdom of God, and all these things shall be added to you."[38] Being in the world yet not of it requires turning to the Spirit first in all questions of truth, and asking, "Is this of God?" If something can't be linked to Spirit as a manifestation of Good, then it has no power. Don't worry about it.

There is even a deeper understanding of this principle of completeness, which is "I *am* the meat; I *am* the bread and the wine." When you are in the world but not of it, you can practice the principle of completeness in the realization that *I have all*. All that the Father has is mine. Yet, there is a greater understanding in knowing that in your experience of oneness, *I am that*–I am the sun and moon and stars; I am that which constitutes my good. When you see beauty, harmony, joy, and fulfillment in the world, realize that *you* are that. There is only one I, and when you recognize Its manifestations in whatever circumstance, know that you can never be separated from It. Though it appears to be coming through another, bless that manifestation, for it is God incarnate. You will come to realize that it is your experience also.

DETACHMENT

Bring the Wholeness of God into Your Experience by Letting Go of Human Concepts

The principle of detachment makes some people uncomfortable. They think of detachment as being indifferent, as being cut off and not part of life. Orthodoxy has interpreted the flesh as sinful, something we suffer until we are redeemed. In that belief, it is only after we die that we experience heaven. Mysticism teaches that the spiritual realm is here, within us, and that we experience its fruits to the degree that we are detached from material concepts. In the Bible, St. Paul says that we must "die daily." In Corinthians, he talks about the nature of death, and its relationship to spiritual living. He talks about two beings: The natural man and the man who has his being in Christ. This may all sound a little religious to mystical students, but Paul understood the nature of spiritual living and how to get there.

One of the greatest and most difficult statements Paul made[39] was "this corruptible must put on incorruption, and this mortal must put on immortality." In his rather arcane way, Paul tells us how to do that. First, he uses the resurrection of the Christ to assure us that this transition can be made. "If Christ be not raised, your faith is vain, ye are yet in your sins." Let's put this in contemporary language. It is interesting that Paul is talking about Christ, not Jesus. He is reminding us that it is the indwelling spirit of God that transforms us, not our human identity or some other human being. As mortal man, we can no more put on immortality than we can crawl back into our mother's womb and be born again. But, the Christ within us *is* immortal and incorrupt, and always has been. The Christ is another name for our spiritual axis. The Christ reconciles the human trinity with the divine, discarding concepts that appear to separate us from experiencing the spiritual kingdom. We are in "sin" when we function from the material perspective. That sense of sin, which gives material appearances–even the appearance of death–their sense of power, dies in us the moment the Christ rises. Our prayers are not in vain when we understand the resurrection as our individual awareness of the Christ consciousness within–that spiritual axis that is always one with our spiritual source. Putting on "incorruption" and "immortality" is a conscious act that we must take by grabbing hold of our spiritual axis within, and letting the activity of love reveal who we really are. Once this Christ consciousness is realized, it is outwardly manifested to meet the need of the moment, just as it manifested in Jesus as his resurrection.

Next, Paul talks about our body in the context of the resurrection. "For as in Adam all die, even so in Christ shall all be made alive." This is a promise based on the omnipotence of our spiritual axis. This promise depends on our "dying" to the material concept of self that we entertain, not only about our own self, but also about everybody else. As we realize that the appearance world is not true and as we become detached enough that we don't want to change it, we become alive in spiritual consciousness. This does not mean that the world we experience is illusion, but our *perception* of it through our mental conditioning shows us a world that appears to us according to our beliefs. If we struggle to change the appearance, we miss the Reality that already exists right where we are. But, when we detach ourselves from the appearance, whether the appearance is failing health, failing relationships or an empty pocketbook, and we let the Christ come alive in us, His love lifts us out of the problem. Additionally, we detach ourselves from the good appearances so that the activity of God, manifesting as individual good, is not limited by personal sense. This takes our joy and fulfillment out of the realm of concept and into the eternal activity of love. The most difficult part of this principle is not letting the appearance gain a sense of power in our consciousness. And, we can do that in this way:

First, we **impersonalize** the problem and remove all material cause by *nullifying karma.*

Next, we **withdraw judgment** from the appearance and identify with our spiritual Source.

From there, we can **detach** ourselves from any "draw" the problem has, either through desire or fear.

Now we are *dead* to this world, awaiting the resurrection. "And as we have borne the image of the earthly, we shall also bear the image of the heavenly." The earthly image is the "Adam man." You might say that the Adam man is the ego, filled with concepts and viewing the world from a personal perspective. As soon as that Adam man dies, the Christ is known. This act of detachment gives us a new perspective on the world, and what we saw through the conditioned mind as the dualistic nature of life with its good and bad, up and down, loses its attraction. It is like watching a movie in which the story suddenly goes flat. You are no longer attached to the character's struggle and you begin to perceive different aspects of the movie–the lighting, the camera work, the direction. You are no longer being acted upon from without and being drawn into the drama, but are now conscious of your reactions and understand what is motivating them. Similarly, mystical awakening reveals what is going on behind the scenes of this world. It shows us that that Kingdom is infinitely more fulfilling and attractive than the realm of human concept. What is more amazing is that when you experience your spiritual oneness, your life begins to manifest the Christ, bringing you a world of beauty, harmony and abundance. In that sense, we bear the image of the heavenly.

Finally, Paul tells us this transformation takes place "in a moment, in the twinkling of an eye." This means that there is no process involved in spiritual wholeness. It is like the ones and zeros. When you are a zero, you are complete in your spiritual state; and, when you are a one, you carry the material baggage of whatever concepts you still cling to. When you are detached, you are ready to meet any problem from a spiritual standpoint.

When we are detached from this world through the spirit, we have no interest in proving ourselves right, or in trying to convince others to accept our sense of truth. Jesus tells the story of a man who felt another mistreated him. In Biblical terms, he had been "trespassed against." The man asked the Master how to correct this wrong. Jesus told him to go alone to the trespasser and work things out. If the trespasser listens to you, you will have gained a brother. One of the greatest forms of attachment is an unresolved wrong. If it can be resolved, you are free. "But, if the trespasser won't listen," the Master continues, "take two or three others with you as witnesses. If you still can't resolve it, take it to the authorities." But, Jesus cautions here, "What you bind on earth you bind in heaven, and what you loose on earth you loose in heaven."[40] When you understand that heaven and earth are states of consciousness, you will be quick to forgive, and you will let go of seeking justice in exchange for the peace and wholeness of spiritual oneness.

Omnipotence

~

Not by might, nor by power, but by My spirit…

ZECHARIAH 4:6

In the "Star Wars" era, "the force" became a popular alternative term for spiritual power. The term "force" didn't define what kind of power it was, but those receptive to the force could use it. Somehow its undefined nature and availability gave the force more appeal than the religious idea of omnipotence, or all power. People liked the idea that with the proper training and attitude you could have free access to this power. There was no need for an intermediary; you just needed an aptitude and a willingness to work at it. We all want to feel that we are connected to something greater than ourselves, and it is comforting to think that we have an invisible force with us in our time of need.

Much of the orthodox religious world acknowledges God as omnipotent and then, without thinking, gives all kinds of power to evil and asks God to overcome it. Or, they explain disasters that have no personal evil cause as "acts of God "or "the will of God." It's as if we are being punished for some unknown sin. But, neither of these ideas represents the nature of "omnipotence" as defined by the mystic.

The idea of "the force" doesn't hold up spiritually because in the context of the Star Wars stories, the force can be used for good or evil. And, it would seem that it is always the evil use of power that is most dramatic. Darth Vader and Seth were far more popular than Luke Skywalker and Obi-Wan Kenobi. In orthodoxy, Satan, the fallen angel, has somehow grown to rival God in his power over human beings; that which cannot be ascribed to the Devil becomes the unexplainable will of God. Yet, in God there is no evil–all spiritual literature affirms this. God is too pure to behold iniquity. Any power that could have an opposite is not omnipotent. And, so we are back to what every other principle has shown: There is only God and nothing else.

To make spiritual revelation practical in our lives, we need to reconcile the apparent world of two powers in the context of spiritual truth. All spiritual truth is absolute. Omnipotence (*all power*) rules out any other power. It is complete and universal, and has the same characteristics as Oneness–It is without opposite. Its application is infinite in expression, and It functions as law to those who realize Its authority.

The authority of spiritual truth has three facets represented by the Holy Trinity. As we touched on earlier, the original trinity in the early Christian community stood for the power of life as represented by father, mother, and child. Even today, in some metaphysical churches, God is referred to as *Father-Mother God*. In today's orthodox church, the trinity is Father, Son, and Holy Spirit. At an individual level, the trinity is soul, mind, and body. The mystical representation of the trinity is Life, Truth, and Love; and, the spiritual source is Omnipotence, Omniscience, and Omnipresence. Let's see how these apply to living the middle path.

Omnipotence = Life = Soul = Father
Omniscience = Truth = Mind = Holy Spirit (Mother)
Omnipresence = Love = Body = Son (or Child)

The male nature, or Father, represents power. Life is omnipotent. Witness the blade of grass breaking through concrete. The power of life cannot be stopped. Life is the soul of the universe, including all mankind. Joel revealed that God is the soul of man.

Soul, whether in a person, an animal, or the universe itself, is God–the source of all Good and of all power, and it is unchangeable. In the traditional trinity, man's soul changed as the Holy Spirit filled it. But, this cannot happen if God is the Soul of man. As we accept God as the substance of all form, then it is our bodies that change as we experience the Holy Spirit. Ultimately, body is spiritual, the perfect manifestation of God, or God appearing as form. That form functions in this world according to the activity of the mind, which is the vehicle for the Holy Spirit. The Holy Spirit is our female nature, that part of us receptive to the activity of the Father. And, to the degree our mind is pure, it opens the door to My Kingdom.

If the soul is God incarnate, the Word made flesh, then it is through the mind that we become aware of this. When the mind is in a state of stillness, we can experience the presence of God within. The mind is the key. As Paul said, "Let this *mind* be in you that was in Christ Jesus."[41] A mind filled with the Holy Spirit reveals your soul as God and brings your body into mystical union. In other words, mind is the transparency for awareness that either aligns you with God, the Reality of all life, or aligns you with the material world, which is but a concept of the Real. Soul is the omnipotence of God expressed as the individual. It is the law of life. It is the rock upon which all material appearances crash.

The female nature, or Mother, is wisdom. From ancient times it was always believed that omniscience flowed through the female, the receptive nature. She is the truth of being; the source of all knowledge; the expression of creativity and invention. This female nature is our mind in its unconditioned state. As is known to most metaphysical students, a mind imbued with truth is a law of harmony unto our being. Seeing the world with an unconditioned mind, a mind free of human belief and judgment, is to see the spiritual source behind the form. It is to see the Christ, or the soul, in another and recognize the One. The unconditioned mind is the agent of discernment. It reveals the truth that sets us free.

The Son, or the child, is love. It is the expression of life and truth. It is omnipresent as the individual manifestation of the One.

It is omnipresent in that we always have a body, and that body is infinite and one, as well as individual and specific. The Son is manifest as the form necessary to function in this dimension, and as such is the temple of the "living God." When this spiritual nature of body is realized, its manifestation is whole, perfect, and the Word made flesh. In this state, we remain as we were created in the image and likeness of Father-Mother God.

The mind and body are the variable aspects in living between the two worlds. The conditioned mind appears as the mortal body. The unconditioned mind reveals the incorporeal nature of individual being. Soul is unchangeable. Experiencing the soul transforms our perception of who we are. It takes us out of our conditioned beliefs into a state of illumination, and that transformation permits the body to reflect spiritual perfection. In other words, your physical body–its health, mobility, and freedom–are a product of your mental state. If your mind is clear and attuned to your spiritual Self, you function under spiritual law and experience freedom. If your mental state is personalized to your ego and physical appearance, you experience what has been called the "unholy trinity."

The "unholy trinity" is time, space, and persona. It appears to be the power source for the material world. It begins with the ego, which personalizes your experience according to your beliefs and concepts of what constitutes good and evil, right and wrong, and cause and effect. When you were born, you entered the conceptual world as a human being. You were seen as a baby, a "new life" coming into a family conditioned by its beliefs of good and evil. Even though your soul is intact, and you are not separated from God, others now see you as flesh and blood; and, that appearance begins to veil your spiritual oneness. This initial judgment forms a concept in the mind of your parents, and material conditioning begins. You are defined by gender, race, and human ancestry. Adults judge your new life by how it appears, and reinforce a sense of separation from your spiritual source. You feel this, and begin to make your own judgments about what has power and what does not; that is, where love and safety are and where they are not. Your parents and family possessively love the "I" that is born. They worry about your well being, fear for your future, and teach you to protect yourself from danger. Soon all have lost sight of the "I" as eternal and incorporeal.

This is the pattern that gives power to the world of effect. This pattern of judgment is based upon a personal ego, rather than seeing the omnipotence of soul. The conditioned observer believes that life exists in a specific place, beginning at a certain time, with a particular kind of body and personality. The world is then perceived through specific conditioning as to who and what to love or hate, rather than by knowing the truth that *I* exists in the consciousness of God–inseparable from all spiritual creation and one with friend and enemy, alike. Conditioned observers believe that life moves through time from birth to death. They are fearful of the unknown and base their actions on the experiences of the past. In reality, the life we live, the life we *are*, is immortal in the *nowness* of God. The journey through this world, the world of time and space, is the Adam dream.

In order to live between two worlds and walk the middle path–which is to live in the omnipotence of God–you must have some awareness of the source of material belief. It is usually through ignorance that you fall victim to the limitations, the pain and suffering of material cause and effect. When you don't know that there is a higher authority to life than the laws of this world, you are subject to these laws and all that they bring with them–the good with the evil. That is why Joel Goldsmith was so insistent on teaching the nature of material sense. Without the ability to see the conceptual nature of material appearance in the light of spiritual revelation, there can be no healing. If you experience the spiritual Presence and do not realize that It is a law of peace and harmony, *here and now*, in whatever situation you happen to be in, you miss the point of spiritual living.

Applying the principle of omnipotence to your life takes you out of the ego sense of might and into the humility of oneness. It is from that awareness that you can apply the commandment to love your enemies and resist not evil. If mankind were to follow that commandment, which is the lawful application of the principle of omnipotence, it would instantly bring peace to the world. Loving your enemies and not resisting evil is not a capitulation to tyranny, but an application of spiritual freedom. It can be demonstrated, individually, to create a peaceful life. And, if enough people practice this principle, it can transform the world.

The story of Elijah dramatizes the nature of this principle. Elijah was aware of the inner nature of the spiritual world, but he wanted to bring that awareness to the world through a show of material power. His preaching alienated the king, and Elijah was forced to hide in the wilderness and then flee to a foreign country. During that time, he experienced the ever-present nature of God. Ravens brought him food. A widow took him in, and Elijah brought her son back to life. Elijah had experience in the spiritual realm, but the one thing he didn't realize was the nature of omnipotence. He thought he could bring God power into the world and eliminate evil and oppression. He had witnessed the power of God, and he thought that if only "the masses" could see the power of God in action, they would accept His omnipotence. But, mass consciousness depends on judging after appearances. Mass consciousness is easily manipulated by ego gratification, which just perpetuates the sense of separation from one's spiritual nature and reinforces the sense of power in the material world. Still, Elijah was determined to show the world the power of God and convince the masses to return to the God of Abraham–the one omnipotent deity.

He challenged the priests of Baal, a rival god, to a contest. They were to make a sacrifice to their god, and Elijah would make a sacrifice to his. Whichever god consumed his sacrifice first would be declared the only powerful and omnipotent God. Elijah taunted the priests saying, "Where is your god? Is he sleeping? Has he forsaken you?" No man-made god appeared to consume the offering made to it. Then, Elijah called to his god, Jehovah. But, Jehovah is really another concept; a *personalized* version of the Infinite Invisible discovered by Moses. This misconception gave power to something "out there," rendering man insignificant and impotent in the face of the almighty. However, Elijah believed this was where his power came from. He had felt this power course through his body and bring the widow's son back to life. He had seen this power direct the birds to bring him food. Certainly this was what God-power was all about. So, in his belief, Elijah brought down thunder and lightning from heaven. He was the agent calling to earth this great power to awe the people into believing. And, the lightning hit the offering and consumed it. The crowds ran in fear. The losing priests called for Elijah's death. Nobody converted to the worship of Jehovah–they feared him more than ever now–while Elijah fled to the hills frightened for his life.

Alone in a cave, humbled by what he had experienced, Elijah pondered what had gone wrong. He couldn't figure out why his demonstration of God's power didn't bring all mankind to worship Him. While in the cave, Elijah experienced an earthquake, and God said he wasn't in the earthquake. Then there was a fire and a storm, and God said he wasn't in them. Then there was silence. In that state of consciousness, Elijah realized that silence is Omnipotence. Stillness and silence is spiritual union, Oneness. There is nothing more powerful than the Silence. When you realize that, you are free from the apparent power of this world. You see disease, conflict, and all destructive forces as products of the belief that there is power in material cause and effect. When you enter that Silence you realize that those forces are not power. Only God is power, and God is not a power over anything. God is omnipotent–the *only* power. What appears as power, if it is not of God, dissolves in the presence of the Silence. What is of God has no destructive action.

NON-POWER

Withdrawing Power from the World of Effect is the Basis for Spiritual Healing

I remember my parents discussing spiritual principles with someone who held only to the absolute. To him, everything in this world was not real. If someone was suffering from a disease, it was not real. If someone was struggling with raising a family and disciplining a child, he thought that correcting bad behavior was unnecessary because God was all in all. To him, there was no bad behavior and there was no evil. The frustration of trying to live in the absolute while dealing with everyday problems can drive you mad. Yet, absolute truth exists universally. God *is* omnipotent. God *is* ever-present. Evil does not exist in God. How can there be another power if God is omnipotent?

I heard a story that characterizes the lengths one will go to in an effort to deny what's going on around him. A man comes to work one morning and his colleague asks him how his mother is doing. The man says that his mother is doing fine for her age, but she thinks she's slowing down a bit. A few weeks later the colleague, again, asks the man about his mother. He answers that she thinks she is sick. Another week goes by and the colleague wants to know how his mother is doing. The man pauses a bit and then replies, "My mother thinks she's dead."

We must reconcile ourselves with life, as we know it, in all of its dimensions–pleasure, beauty, and fulfillment, along with pain, disappointment, and suffering. As we have seen, we can't reconcile these from the ego sense of life. We can't pretend a state of consciousness we haven't experienced. From the ego point of view, we are limited in our actions, and even more limited in originality to solve our problems. As Paul said, we *must* put on immortality. That means the only way we can come under spiritual law is by taking hold of our spiritual axis and letting that divine Activity manifest Itself in us. We are not saying that the material world doesn't exist. We aren't saying that it's all an illusion, and we aren't telling the person crying in pain that the pain isn't real. We are shifting our perception to the spiritual, and from that point of view, we realize that there is no power in the realm of effect while we are experiencing spiritual consciousness.

As Joel Goldsmith says on a tape, *"Some teachings claim that we are completely perfect and spiritual now, and therefore all of this (treatment/prayer) would be unnecessary. In our spiritual identity that's true. But, it certainly isn't true of our humanhood. And, it's our humanhood, or to our humanhood, that we are trying to bring light, so that we may outgrow this humanhood. But, just denying that you're a human being and stating that you are already perfect, and already spiritual, and already have the mind of God, is a form of 'Coueism.' You're claiming something for yourself that you haven't demonstrated."*[42]

How do we "withdraw power" from the world of cause and effect? It is impossible while we are still in the world of cause and effect. The only way to withdraw power from material sense is to shift our perspective into the spiritual and apply the principles found on the Gate to Illumination. When we realize the non-power of material effect, we instantly connect to our spiritual axis and live under spiritual law. Here are the steps:

Impersonalize – realize that there is no person *on* whom or *through* whom evil, in any form, can function. Evil, or any destructive power, is a concept based on human history and it can be dropped from consciousness the moment one realizes that human history has nothing to do with the expression of God. "God's rain falls on the just and the unjust."[43]

Withdraw judgment – refuse to judge the appearance either good or evil. To judge according to material belief condemns you to the circumstances inherent in the appearance. If you can erase whatever form a concept takes in your mind, you have the opportunity to see the person, or the situation, as it truly is; either as a spiritual manifestation, a child of God, or as nothing at all because it has no foundation in Spirit. When you identify the truth of a person from a spiritual perspective, you see their universal, spiritual core. And, *you* discover the truth about your Self.

Detach yourself from any and all concepts you observe, whether they are of yourself or another. Then, you can bear witness to the truth because you no longer have any connection to the concept. What you are facing is an appearance, or illusion, without any substance, law, or action, and you cannot be fooled into reacting.

Now where is the power? It's not in anything outside of *your own perception*. It's not in the person, or the situation, or the circumstance you are seeing because all of that has been brought into the light of Spirit through applying the principles to the situation. You have withdrawn power from effect, and therefore withdrawn power from any discordant, destructive, and limiting appearance. Where is the power? It is within *your consciousness*, and that's the only place where problems can be solved spiritually.

When Jesus stood in front of Pontius Pilate, he was standing in front of the most powerful person in his world, a provincial governor in the Roman Empire who had absolute power over the people in his province. There were many other forces at work in the Holy Land at that time, but it was Pilate who had the last word. So, when Jesus told Pilate that he could have no power over him except what came from above, it was shocking to all who heard it. Many laughed. Some, however, understood what Jesus was setting into motion. It was the destruction of the personal sense of power–that sense of power doesn't back down. It is not humble. It supports itself through manipulation and appeasement, and through deception and force. It hates to admit failure. It does everything it can to survive and increase its influence. In his awareness that the personal concept of ego lacks power in the face of spiritual realization, Jesus stepped out into the infinite realm of Consciousness to demonstrate that material power of any kind is impotent in the presence of God realized. He had already shown the impotence of disease, sin, and lack. He healed the sick, forgave the sinner, and fed the multitudes. Now was the time to prove that even death was not a power to one who has his being in God. His resurrection dissolved the power of death and showed us that our spiritual nature, when realized, has dominion over our material concept of life.

The result of Jesus' full demonstration of his Christhood was a level of individual freedom that the world had never before seen. His resurrection nullified the power that material cause and effect had over the world. Once a spiritual principle is realized and demonstrated, it becomes a tangible part of human experience. Resurrection is still just an idea for most of the world, but so was the idea that man could fly until the Wright Brothers perfected the idea. Those of us working with spiritual principles are still perfecting the way to bring the Truth into our daily experience, and to the degree that we witness healing of the body, mind, and "purse," we break down the hypnotism of material power. The Adam dream, under which mankind has been living, breaks down as we awaken to spiritual law.

Now, if you have a more scientific perspective of the world and can't make the correlation between the Christian resurrection and individual freedom, I can put it another way. You know from Genesis that creation is spiritual. The manifestation of the sun, moon, stars, earth, and all that the earth supports begins in Spirit. If the "big bang" is the beginning of the universe, where did it take place? If it was in a void, the void can be a synonym for God. You could say the "big bang" took place in Consciousness, in infinite awareness, and in the eternal moment. Looking back into time, that which evolved did so under specific principles. Not all of those principles are known yet, but from what is known, different laws account for different aspects of creation. The infinite relationships in space follow their own laws, and they all seem to be in proper order, no matter how chaotic they might seem to the human mind. The evolution of life on earth followed another set of laws, and those laws seem to bind life to specific parameters.

For us to live, we need an atmosphere of oxygen, water, and some sort of food. Underlying all of this is another set of laws that science can't define because they can't be measured; and, those are the laws of Spirit. They include the whole of creation, and come into effect when they are realized. They are communicated by the poet or the mystic, and they are understood in the silence of your Soul. Often, when these expressions of Spirit are collected into a religion, they lose their individual effectiveness. But, when we look at the core demonstrations of the illumined men and women who defined spiritual principles, we find a valid way to experience an aspect of life hidden by the ignorance of the accepted belief about life and death.

Jesus took away the authority of the material belief structure. He opened the door to a new science, a new discipline that breaks the limitation of sensory observation and the logic based on the premise that material cause and effect are the only powers in the world. No longer is life dependent on the body. It is the body that is dependent on Spirit for all of its activities. No longer is mind limited to the knowledge collected though material observation and experience. The mind is the vehicle for spiritual transcendence, for grasping the nature of creation in all of its facets. And, a life is not defined by the number of years in this world, but by its realization of spiritual reality. Knowing this spiritual reality frees you from material limitations. But, knowing the Truth is not about what has been written or what you can recall–the so called "letter of truth." It is about *experiencing* the presence of God in the silence of your Soul. That experience removes the fear embedded by the ego, and actually takes you out of the personal sense of life into the manifestation of your spiritual being. But, as Jesus showed, you must be willing to give up your material concept of life to experience the oneness and omnipotence of God. What greater joy can there be than to live in spiritual freedom?

Omniscience

~

I am the way, the truth and the life.

JOHN 14:6

There is a fine line between chaos and illumination. The reasoning mind wants to put everything in linear, logical order, progressing from A to B to C. The illumined mind is not linear, and experiences the center and circumference simultaneously. In its common use, the term "circumference" refers to the boundary of a circle, but in mysticism we talk about the "circle of eternity." It is that which is without beginning or end. Therefore, in the non-linear illumined mind, one is aware, simultaneously, of the micro, the center of all life within, and the macro, the infinite manifestation of life. This totality of life is eternal. The infinite within is the unseen realm in which all form exists in its spiritual archetype. This realm is not chaos, as we touched on earlier, but *rather* it is spiritually defined creation existing in the Infinite Invisible and available for us to know in the consciousness of Omniscience. Our experience in this realm brings those spiritual ideas relative to our individual experience into manifestation. In fact, our experience of any one of the great principles in this book opens us to the experience of all of them. In our experience of Oneness, we are one with all spiritual form and identity. In the *now moment* we are spiritually complete, and our realization of this brings us everything necessary for our joy and fulfillment. Our realization of omnipotence removes power from the world of material cause and effect. And, our awareness of omniscience fills us with spiritual understanding. We *know* that God is omnipresent, and we can experience unconditioned love.

From the invisible spiritual realm comes the understanding of the infinite nature of life without the limited concepts inherent in the Adam dream. Though we see and experience the physical nature of life through our mind and body, as we develop our spiritual faculties, the omniscience of Being begins to reveal the truth behind the appearance. This comes through our Soul. When the truth and the appearance don't correspond, we make a judgment–a righteous judgment–and let our inner activity of omniscience "see through" the appearance. Even if we can't physically discern the truth, our confidence in our inner spiritual Self keeps fear away. This attitude facilitates our shift from the appearance world into the omniscience of spiritual Reality. It lets the Christ within define our experience, and with the Christ-Peace, we are assured that any appearance of harm or discord of any nature has no power. This attitude puts us in God Consciousness, and regardless of appearances, peace and harmony will prevail. That is spiritual law.

On the other hand, if we accept an appearance without question, we give it power and we function under its jurisdiction. Our ability to choose between the spiritual and the material is not a function of the intellect or our personal sense of ego. It is our inherent spiritual dominion coming into our awareness as an act of grace. It really is a shift in our cognitive ability. Spiritual revelation comes through Soul. In popular culture when people feel this spiritual connection, they talk about "coming from the heart" rather than from the intellect. This heart level is really our soul connection, and when we learn to function from this level of consciousness, we find life unfolding through us from the divine Source. When we have the wisdom to take any problem or situation deep into the spiritual realm, we discover that our higher Self takes over. The ego self is a subjective reality, and once the concepts upon which it is built fade, ego power and material effect also fade. In their place our spiritual nature reveals life as an activity of God. That is our Reality.

Omniscience, or Divine Wisdom, reveals spiritual Reality. This revelation is enlightenment, or illumination. The illumined individual is one who constantly looks for the truth behind the appearance. Our spiritual nature doesn't exist in the limited world of material concepts. That would be impossible because our spiritual nature is eternal. The concepts we hold of life–how it should be lived and how it works –are mental impositions on the spiritual reality that is all around us and within us. To give expression to spiritual reality you need to step out of this world and become one with the Infinite Invisible. This is the crux of living between two worlds, or walking the middle path. At this point in your spiritual development, you are aware of the spiritual realm and must deal with everyday life from your Soul, rather than from your mind. Here's how it is done.

As you practice living in the *now* and allow all material beliefs to be examined through your spiritual insight, you begin to understand the nature of this world and its relationship to Reality. Using the principle of omniscience, you bring yourself under spiritual law. Actually, as you let go of your attachment to the personal sense of ego, all spiritual principles kick in automatically as an activity of Soul–your higher Self, or Christ. With this knowledge you become an observer of material cause and effect, rather than one who tries to manipulate it or get rid of it. You try not to engage in that power structure. You are a witness, not the judge or jury, and certainly not the plaintiff or defendant. In whatever situation you find yourself, you detach yourself from the problem, the conflict, or disease, and refer those appearances to a higher authority–the Christ within you. That authority, whether you call it Christ, or Brahman, or Self, is a mediator. It is unconditioned, so It sees the problem without forming any material conclusions and It reveals the truth. You don't fight or resist the appearance, or engage in any kind of mental argument with the problem. As I've said before, you can't solve a problem spiritually on the level of the problem. To fight or resist material appearances draws you back into the conceptual level of life, and you lose sight of the spiritual reality right there. Letting material concepts fall into that deep well of spiritual consciousness removes the burden from you to have to overcome evil from a personal perspective, and it shifts the responsibility to the omniscience of the Infinite Invisible. That level of knowledge, which you have in your realization of omniscience, corrects the misconception or reveals it to be nothing.

Having done that, you rest in the presence of Love. As an activity of Love–and remember, all these principles work in concert–Omniscience reveals the following:

You recognize your relationship of oneness with the Infinite.

The *now-ness* of spiritual activity keeps you centered.

You realize the completeness of a spiritual idea, unaltered by material concept.

You experience the omnipotence of the inner Silence.

It's interesting to note how revelation comes. Sometimes, it comes "out of the blue" without a lot of analyzing or thought. At other times, we see a new pattern, a new relationship, in the problems we have been working to solve.

Omniscience cannot be divorced from the intellect, any more than the body can be divorced from the mind. In other words, living from a spiritual perspective doesn't shut off your awareness of your human selfhood or the world around you. It brings into your experience aspects of spiritual reality which, when understood, alter your perception of everyday life. All of us live on many levels. We are one person to our families, perhaps another to our acquaintances, and still another to the general public. The insight omniscience brings does not remove you from these worlds. It just puts these relationships into a spiritual perspective.

A scientist friend and I were talking about how the language defining spiritual living has changed over the years. Words are always limited in defining experience. As a surfer who rode the big waves on Oahu's North Shore, I never could convey the experience, verbally, to someone who hadn't experienced it. With a fellow surfer it was a nod, a smile, or a few simple expressions of "wow," "cool," "awesome," and we understood each other because we had a common experience. In the 1960s when Joel Goldsmith taught the fourth dimension of consciousness, he was coming off the belief that reality had only three dimensions–up, down, and sideways. Back then, to call something "3-D" meant that it was real. Since we got most of our news and entertainment from media that was two-dimensional and flat, studios tried making movies more real by showing them in 3-D, but, you needed glasses to create the illusion. So, when Mr. Goldsmith talked about the forth dimension, he was talking about a reality that was not in the realm of the senses.

Our three-dimensional concepts masked the deeper reality known to mystics. At the beginning of the 1960s–that decade of unprecedented change–Mr. Goldsmith said that nothing in the three-dimensional world was as it seemed. The material world wasn't real, and it could be changed. To present the spiritual dimension where joy, fulfillment, and freedom were untouched by human concept, Mr. Goldsmith used the term "the fourth dimension of consciousness." What my friend pointed out, though, is that a dimension is a term of measurement. Einstein needed another dimension to explain his theory of relativity, and he theorized the fourth dimension as time. Physicists now theorize many more dimensions based on their measurements in the sub-atomic world.

The mystical sense of life cannot be measured. We are used to calling it a "dimension" because it seems to be another world; a parallel universe, or state of being, that exists side-by-side with material life, just as the quantum world exists along side the Newtonian world of classical physics. But, in physics, the quantum laws don't mix with the Newtonian laws; in order to understand either world takes the knowledge of both specific sets of laws. The mystical experience is another perception of the world. As Joel Goldsmith put it, "The world is new to every soul when Christ has entered into it."[44] When the mystical world opens to us, we see as the Christ sees. We have learned from scripture that "to see as Christ sees" requires "righteous judgment" and forgiveness. Illumination is the spiritual perception we develop by becoming aware of our spiritual nature and recognizing the Christ presence when we feel it.

This can never be an ego thing. (What I am referring to here is the personal sense of the one Ego, which is our Self seen through the prism of human conditioning.) Once the ego begins to believe it is spiritual, that person has problems. That is why most religions stress humility. "If I bear witness to myself, I bear witness to a lie."[45] Yet, "I and the Father are one."[46] As we watch the spiritual nature in us come forth, and as we let it live our life, we enter a state of grace. This is not easy to do. We are taught from an early age to take possession of our lives and be masters of our own fate, and *that* conditioning makes it difficult to let go. The moment we realize that "I am Spirit, and Spirit is the reality of who I am," it is possible to let go of the personal sense of ego.

This is a good place to review the mind-body-ego relationship in the context of Omniscience. The all-knowing aspect of Spirit doesn't enter the human dream. We can never bring Omniscience into the dream, but we can awaken to its activity and understand how "this world" affects us, and how it loses power as we experience the Spirit within. You are probably aware of the various metaphysical movements and books that are quite popular. One book states that it reveals the ancient secret of the "law of attraction." The law of attraction postulates that what you hold in your mind is manifested in your body and experience. That can be a disturbing idea if you are suffering and think that somehow your thinking caused it. I can tell you that from a mystical perspective, thought has no power. But, it can appear to be a force in the human scene. So, how do we deal with that?

To the degree that we accept the belief that material good and evil have power, we live under their jurisdiction, even though right here, in the *now*, spiritual reality exists in all of its glory and splendor. To experience the Kingdom of Heaven here on earth, we must change our perception. We must first recognize, and then acknowledge, the spiritual nature of creation in consciousness. We can't do that with our five physical senses because they are locked into the realm of appearances. We have to let the divine Wisdom within us change our perception. To do that, we let go of our human conditioning; that is, what we think about our person, what we hold onto in our mind, and how we react to events in the world. This means we stop judging life through our human beliefs of good and evil. When our sensory world is testifying to pain and suffering, or to war and hatred, we reconcile these discrepancies to what we know of Truth in consciousness through the Christ, our higher Self.

As individuals, we are one with all spiritual form and expression, and we are also unique–God appearing as individual being in infinite form and variety. We experience our oneness and our individuality through the mind that is free of material conditioning. In metaphysics we are taught that there is only one mind. From a material perspective that seems ridiculous. Each one of us seems to possess a personal, unique mind. But, what if the uniqueness of our mind was not so unique? What if there is a universal conditioning that functions in every one of us? What if we discover that something we thought was unique to us wasn't so unique; that many people in many cultures exhibited the same trait? Would we begin to let go of our personalized sense of mind? Hopefully we would. But, this universal conditioned state of mind, common to all of us, is aggressive and is the tool of the personal sense of ego. To the degree that we disengage from the personal sense of ego and its connection to the conditioned mind, we begin to perceive life through the lens of Omniscience and discover that the influence of material conditions decreases.

For spiritual students, the awareness of Consciousness based on oneness shifts us out of the mind/body/personality sense of being and into the realization that mind and body exist <u>*in*</u> consciousness; that our identity is spiritual, not material. From the mystical perspective, our world is the manifestation of Spirit–though seen through human conditioning. In Reality, all that is, is spiritual, inseparable in form and substance from its creator. That includes all of us. We are individual beings, indivisible from our creator. Yet, we experience this world through our senses, our feelings, and our accumulated knowledge. These concepts color the manifested creation of God with the patina of material belief–a belief that evil is a power, and that it somehow contends with God for control of the material world. These false concepts are not power in our experience to the degree that we realize the Truth. It is not how much we fight, or how much we know. Spiritual freedom, and the fullness of joy, comes to us through realizing the presence of God within.

All the ideas, theories, and inventions that have been manifested over the eons exist in this universal mind. Individuals pick up these ideas from the universal mind and, if they have the means and intelligence to express them, they give the world its music and art, its commerce, its law, and its political structure. Not all of these ideas have been good for mankind because the universal mind is conditioned by human belief. But, this same mind in an unconditioned state, free of material judgment, is the mind that was in Christ Jesus. Again, the "mind that was in Christ Jesus" is not something formed in the brain of Jesus of Nazareth. It is Omniscience functioning through the illumined individual.

In our times of transition, we seem to be *two* selves. One of these selves we have known all our lives as our personal ego. The other one is less well defined. It seems to be more of a feeling that brings joy; but, when it is defined and personalized by the ego, it disappears. This is perplexing. The more we want to *own* the spiritual part of us on personal terms, the less we experience it. Yet, to let go of the personal ego, and just be in the Spirit, seems like death. The only way to experience the fullness of joy and our spiritual birthright is through a still mind. Our personal ego uses the mind to judge, and when the mind is still, there is no judgment going on, so the personal sense of ego is also still. When you reach this place in meditation, your mind becomes the transparency for spiritual understanding–for Omniscience. It is in this state of being that you begin to see spiritual fruitage in your life.

RESIST NOT EVIL

Stepping Out from the Conditioned Human Mind into the Christ Mind

In the Sermon on the Mount in the Gospel of Matthew, Jesus contrasted the mystical way of life with the moral life based on Mosaic Law. He tells his followers, "You have heard it said of old..." and then replaces the reaction of the ego-based sense of justice with how someone living out from their spiritual axis would respond to events of this world. To respond from our spiritual axis takes a degree of spiritual development, whereby we trust the Infinite Invisible enough to discard our material attachments, and let Spirit function through us. In the Sermon on the Mount, Jesus gives mankind the spiritual laws that will allow one to be in the world yet not of it.

We are blessed according to our attitude and by the degree to which our higher Self maintains dominion over our personal sense of ego. The poor in spirit live in the Kingdom of God; those who mourn are comforted; the meek inherit the earth; and, those who want to know the truth will find it. The merciful will find mercy; the pure in heart will see God; and, the peacemakers are the children of God. We are recognized as the salt of the earth *and* the light of the world. With all of this as our birthright, we should have no problem stepping out from the conditioned human mind into the Christ mind. But, there are very few people on the planet who live this way. So, what does it take to be blessed by the Christ? It takes a pure mind and a willing heart.

Another example of how this works comes, once again, from

our experience with XYZ Company and our commercial property, mentioned in the chapter on Impersonalization. The building had changed over the years with many additions and alterations. It began as two apartments over retail stores. Later, a warehouse was built in the back, and the apartments were turned into offices. Then, the warehouse was connected to the original building and more offices were built. By the time my family acquired the property, it was a mishmash of uses, tenants, and construction. Because of the situation with the XYZ Company, the building was cited as being in violation of some current building codes. We needed an architect to redesign portions of it to meet the code. The architect knew our situation. He thought it unfair that we had to spend money on our well-maintained building, when so many buildings of the same vintage in the same area were in much poorer shape, but not subject to such scrutiny by the city. To him, this was harassment, and he suggested that we sue the city. The family talked it over, and we all decided to follow spiritual law as outlined in the Sermon on the Mount. To do this, successfully, we had to be sure that we held to the Christ mind and did not allow any human sense of loss, anger, resentment, or victim-hood to enter our thought. If we are children of God and wanted to experience the blessings of the Beatitudes, we couldn't slip into the attitude of "you have heard it said of old," which basically is "an eye for an eye," and fighting injustice. Our architect thought the Sermon on the Mount didn't apply to this world. In a way he was right. We can't bring spiritual law into battle with material concepts. But, when we stay connected to our spiritual axis and function from Soul, then "crooked places are made straight" and everyday problems are resolved spiritually.

To maintain the Christ mind, our regime each day was to detach ourselves from any idea or concept that said we were suffering a loss. If our business was an activity of consciousness, then spiritually it was complete. If the idea came that we were being judged unfairly, we replaced that thought with the principle of not judging after appearances but judging righteous judgment. If the people who seemed to cause the problem came into our mind, we impersonalized them; that is, we withdrew any negative agenda from the person, knowing that any personal sense of power is impotent in the light of Truth. That left us dealing with someone who had no conditions attached to him, and we could know that person in the consciousness of One: One self, One life, One expression. The result of this practice kept us living in peace and harmony. It kept us in the consciousness of Spirit, and all the necessary work was done harmoniously.

The human footsteps required that we take out a loan on the building. The money came effortlessly. The reconstruction was ahead of schedule and under budget. The city became very cooperative and "grandfathered in" some of the problems that would have been prohibitively expensive to fix. As soon as we received our occupancy permit, we put the space up for rent and received significantly more in rent than we had before the problem occurred. To see how Spirit functioned in us and through us when we kept our mind stayed on God was a great lesson with a very practical outcome.

A pure mind requires that we do not judge after appearances– no matter if the appearance is a health problem, business problem, or family problem. Instead, we judge righteously, which means we let the omniscience of God function in us to reveal the truth. To have a willing heart requires that we be willing to give up all our material concepts, whether they appear good or not. Are we willing to give up our life to gain our life? If we have experienced the oneness of God in the deep silence of My peace, we know life is eternal, and that we are never separated from that life. Bringing these principles into action will lift us into a healing consciousness. This is how we practice:

1. In addition to "Thou shalt not kill," we abandon hate. The Christ goes to the root of the ego activity, and lifts the individual out of the dualism of that sense of being and into the consciousness of unconditioned love. The Christ brings the intent of the individual in line with spiritual Oneness.

2. In addition to not committing adultery, we realize our fulfillment is in our oneness of spiritual consciousness. There is no need to covet or desire any form of material good; that only diverts us from experiencing the joy and fulfillment that flows out from our spiritual consciousness.

3. Instead of not lying, we are instructed not even to take an oath. The reason for this is that to take sides in a conflict, or even identify with a conflict, takes us out of that unconditioned state of non-judgment and puts us into the world of competing concepts. To be an instrument for healing, we stay "aloof" so that we maintain a pure instrument through which Spirit can operate.

4. Instead of demanding an eye for an eye, we are charged to *resist not evil.* Once we have seen the powerlessness of material effect and realized that the only cause is Spirit, to resist or fight evil draws us back into the realm of the ego, and saps us of our ability to bring Omnipotence into the situation. Problems are never solved on the level of the problem. To withdraw power from the problem in your own perception of it is to let Spirit have its healing activity through you.

When these ideas are established in your consciousness, you will find that you do not react to events on the *appearance* level. You don't react to disease; there is no fear when confronting situations of danger, nor is there concern over the state of the world. Individually you put your government on God's shoulders, taking no thought for yourself, where you live, or how you make a living. You understand the flow of good that functions when you are detached from the world of effect, and you witness Spirit manifesting as all you need.

This fulfills another aspect of living in spiritual freedom: "Seek first the Kingdom of God and all things will be added to you."[47] If we fight evil, even if we think we are doing God's will, we are binding ourselves to the wheel of duality. In the realm of duality, there will always be action and reaction–emotionally, socially, and even on a global scale. There will always be retaliation, and as Gandhi said, "An eye for an eye makes the whole world blind." When we put the Kingdom of Heaven before our ego reactions, we dissolve the obstacles in our way that would cause fear and the results of fear, as we face economic problems, disease, and unhappy situations with the certainty of Spirit backing us up.

Omnipresence

~

Where can I go from your spirit? Where can I flee from your presence?

PSALMS 139:7

Not that long ago, I read that the Voyager spacecraft is now leaving our solar system and entering inner stellar space. It is still sending data back to earth. It takes fourteen hours for the signal to reach us, and another fourteen hours for the scientists in California to get a signal back to make any sort of change. That machine could be traveling among the stars for a billion years! From Voyager's current point of view, our sun is a minor star in the constellation of Orion. None of the sun's planets can be seen. The spacecraft, which is about the size of a Volkswagen, is like a toy in the vast sea of stars swirling around the dark center of our galaxy. Yet, in Consciousness we can be with it instantly! There are no material barriers in the realm of Spirit. Omnipresence cannot be localized, and in the consciousness of Oneness, we are present with all creation since all creation is in Consciousness. The Voyager has never left the consciousness of the scientists who created it. Even as it travels to the outer reaches of space, it is still in the consciousness of those who brought it forth.

Thus it is in the spiritual realm. We were created in God as spiritual manifestations of the One; each an individual, yet each inseparable from the Source. No matter where we are, God is with us. No matter where we are, we are in God–One substance, One source, One presence. Our connection to God is through meditation. As we move into the realm of Spirit through the silence that comes when we are detached from the concepts of this world, our awareness of the Infinite grows. This knowledge removes the fear of the unknown and gives us the courage to put our trust in the Infinite Invisible. As we practice communing with the Spirit this way, we feel that presence of Love wherever we are. Regardless of the situation or where in the world we might be, the presence of God brings peace and understanding. Hostility, danger, and fear do not exist in this Presence, and any appearance of such disappears in the light of Truth.

We have another paradox here. If God is ever present, why is there war, disease, suffering, and pain in the world? It is the same question raised with the principle of Omnipotence: if God is all power, either He allows evil, or He is not truly Omnipotent. This paradox is addressed by the realization that God does not enter the "Adam Dream." Western theology explains this through the story of Adam and Eve, and the fall of man. The Lord God made the world, but gave man free will and man blew it. As a result, man was cast out of paradise and lives a human existence of struggle and pain, and occasional pleasure–none of which is part of God. This paradox comes from the belief that there is a God, and then there is humankind struggling for redemption.

In Eastern thought, this world is an illusion; and, if we had the enlightenment to see that, we would wake up and escape the wheel of karma and suffering–the dream of human existence. We would cease to reincarnate and achieve Nirvana, which is a state of total oneness with all creation.

Contemporary mysticism presents another idea that somewhat combines the Eastern and Western thought. It says that this world is not an illusion or a dream but that our *concept* of it, based on our human conditioning, misrepresents spiritual reality, which is the only Reality. In other words, what we perceive of spiritual Reality is based on a false premise; one founded upon the belief that material cause and effect are power. The appearance of power in matter is a product of material judgment that builds concepts in our mind and reinforces the universal concepts that appear as our world. When we judge righteous judgment and withdraw power from the appearance world, we discover that God is everywhere, within and without, All in all. This doesn't mean that God is *in* material concepts; God is not. God is the presence of stillness that reveals spiritual Reality here and now. When we bear witness to this truth, we break down the appearances that hide spiritual manifestation. Let's see if we can break down this paradox that God is everywhere, but not in material concepts.

The overall Reality of creation–the universe and all it contains; life in all of its manifestation in this world; and whatever other life there might be anywhere–is spiritual. The creative Principle manifests Itself infinitely. Therefore, there can be no place where It is not. This expression of the Infinite is non-dual, One, which makes Spirit the substance of all form. Spirit is eternal, without the limits of time and space. It is complete. Nothing can exist outside of this creation. Everything exists in, and as, Consciousness. Here, we have the alpha and omega, the circle of Eternity, ever within us as we are ever within It. Since we are cognitive beings, we can know this. The awareness of our spiritual self unites us in consciousness to the point where we can say, "I am in all, and all is in me." We experience spiritual Reality in the depths of our soul, beyond thought, in the deep silence of Christ peace. We see and hear and know creation on this level through our developed spiritual senses. This realm is not "make-believe" or fantasy. It is demonstratable and apparent, to anyone with eyes to see and ears to hear.

Mankind has never fallen from Grace. The dualistic nature of the material world is a misconception perpetuated by judging after appearances. We all know its variableness. We are not blind to pain and suffering. Evil appears real and frightening, and we spend lifetimes reinforcing that belief through unquestioning acceptance. We seldom follow the liberating instruction to "judge not according to the appearance, but judge righteous judgment."[48] What is righteous judgment? It certainly has nothing to do with concepts of good and evil. It has nothing to do with human morality. It has to do with knowing what is true (spiritual Reality) and perceiving this world with whatever degree of Truth we have experienced. If we have never experienced the presence of God, we can't judge righteously. If we have a theological concept of God, we cannot judge righteously. Our only freedom is in the experience of the deep Christ peace, the peace that gives understanding. This peace is experienced in stillness, when the mind is free of words, thoughts, concepts, and beliefs; when it is completely empty, in the *now*, and alert.

When this realization comes to you, you will discern the spiritual Presence in all life, but you will not personalize it in any object. You will see a tree and know that you are seeing God in manifestation. However, you will also know that God is not in the physical tree. Your perception of the physical tree is in the realm of concept, just by the fact that you are seeing it with physical eyes. But, at the same time, you can experience that same tree spiritually. You can know its essence, its function, its grand design as part of the planet. The whole earth is the Lord's and the fullness thereof.[49] As long as you don't personalize God into a concept, you can discern through your soul the ever-present nature of God all around you.

The point of living a spiritual life is to be in the presence of God. This is a state of Oneness. Language sometimes hampers this idea in that we seem to be referring to an individual "and" God. This is not true; there is not God "*and*." The omnipresence of God includes everyone. Being in the presence of God is a state of Oneness, not only with our self but with all creation. The truth is that we can never be separated from God. "If I make my bed in hell, thou art there."[50] "Neither life nor death can separate me from God."[51] To be aware of this in the midst of human life not only frees us from the negative influences of the material world, it also frees us from the desire to attach ourselves to the good. We know our being is not dependent upon our physical or mental state, but that it is an activity of Consciousness. Fear leaves us. Death has no sting. The reason for this is the omnipresence of God. Where God is, nothing else can be. Or more clearly, where God is *realized*, nothing but God is manifested. What happens to evil in the presence of God? It doesn't exist. Can we experience this in our daily lives? By all means, yes. Every time you witness a spiritual healing, you are diminishing the apparent power of material beliefs. Every time you experience peace and the forgiveness and reconciliation that come with it, you remove power from material effect.

In modern mysticism, we focus on the underlying spiritual reality and not on the effect it has on our material existence. We strive to know the Kingdom of Heaven and not to go after the "added things." The metaphysics in which I was raised focused on maintaining a harmonious, prosperous human life; and, there is nothing wrong with that. Harmony and prosperity are fruits of the spirit. But, if your focus is only on improving your humanhood, you miss the deeper experience. Christian Scientists have meetings at which they give testimonials about how spiritual understanding heals and transforms. Over the years these meetings established spiritual healing as an accepted way to deal with problems. Healing physical, mental, moral, and emotional problems spiritually became an alternative to traditional medicine; and being cured of cancer, tuberculosis, or heart disease was no longer a *miracle*, but the result of a specific practice. These demonstrations gave credibility to the metaphysical and spiritual movements and paved the way for our practice of spiritual living today.

In today's practice of mysticism, we go to the Source to experience union and witness the transformation from that perspective rather than trying to change the material picture. We don't have to prove Spirit to anyone. We don't have to concentrate on healing the world or bringing a material peace to the nations. By seeking God, we witness all of this without "might or power."[52] It is God's word that brings peace, and that word is the great secret of a life lived in grace. That word is only uttered in the sanctuary of our higher Self (where the personal ego cannot enter) and it is the

Christ within that tells us, "I am that I am"… "Be still and know that I am God."[53] By entering the consciousness of Omnipresence, we are that spiritual expression manifested in all of its bounty, peace, and wholeness.

FEELING THE PRESENCE

Don't Be Hypnotized Out of Omnipresence

When Jesus was tempted by Satan to give power to material effect, he never saw the devil as an adversary who had to be defeated. In the story,[54] Jesus had just left the Jordan River after being baptized by John; and, he was filled with the Holy Spirit. All of the people present had heard the Voice coming from heaven, declaring that Jesus was the Son of God. This was the beginning of his ministry, and it took this kind of declaration and recognition to be ordained. All mystical teachers have gone through a similar ordination. Without the presence of God being felt, and without the spiritual recognition of his followers, a teacher cannot impart the deep mystical Truth. This ordination also takes place within every student following the mystical path. There is a point in your study where you feel that Presence. You receive that blessing of being the beloved child of God. You feel the assurance that God is functioning through you, and your life changes. Once this new you is recognized by anyone, you begin your spiritual ministry. That ministry might only be to yourself, but you are now ready to meet the appearances of this world from your spiritual core.

So, Jesus went out into the wilderness; that is, in consciousness he left the world of words and thoughts, of concepts and beliefs, and was alone. He went to that place where Maimonides said we all must go to "worship the invisible or hidden God alone." Yet, we are never alone for long. Our mind has its moments of complete receptivity where we experience spiritual Oneness, and then the questions come. What is the nature of the world? What is the nature of spirituality? Weighing his revelation of the Christ with all that he had been taught in the temple, Jesus began reconciling the material sense of life with the spiritual. And, the gospel says that the devil was with him the whole time. His spiritual discernment, which gave him the ability to go into the world and heal the sick and raise the dead, was forged in those forty days. He hadn't eaten the whole time, and he was hungry when the devil suggested that he turn a stone into bread. After all, he was now a master and knew the relationship of matter to mind. Why shouldn't he use his power to satisfy himself?

Jesus answered him with a truth. He did not resist or confront Satan. He said, "It is written that man shall not live by bread alone, but by every word of God." Then, Satan took Jesus up to a high mountain, and showed him all the kingdoms of the world, and said that they would be his if he worshiped Satan. Jesus' reply was "Get behind me, for it is written that you should worship only God." Again, he offered no resistance, no arguing or emotional response. Jesus wasn't insulted. He didn't need to change Satan because he knew Satan had no power. Satan is the impulse for our personal sense of ego to assume a power it does not possess. If we give into this impulse, we end up fighting a losing battle, trying to maintain a façade that in reality doesn't exist. Finally, Satan tells Jesus to jump from the pinnacle of the temple, which was the highest point in orthodox understanding, assuring him God's angels would save him from harm. Jesus' dismissal was simple and direct: "You don't tempt God."

This last point is what separates the Christ message from the dogma of the past. Orthodoxy believes that prayer can bring God into the human scene and change it. Mysticism reveals that God is already all-in-all, and that the human scene is a misconception of spiritual reality. If you think you can tempt God into action, even if you are the Son of God, you are still thinking from a material perspective. "This world" is Satan's world, in that it is the product of the material belief that good and evil have power, and that good power is God and evil power is Satan. To live in spiritual freedom, we must know the omnipotence of God, and step out of the dualistic concept of the world in the awareness that God is ever-present. In the recognition of our spiritual consciousness, our union with Spirit, we let the fullness of spiritual creation manifest through us.

Joel Goldsmith gives a great analogy on how we deal with the appearances of this world in his story of the white poodle. It was a story about hypnotism. I had heard this story at a time when hypnotism was popular entertainment, and I remembered going to the Waikiki Shell, Honolulu's première open amphitheater, to watch a great hypnotist perform. The Shell was packed, mostly with college kids and surfers. As part of his act, the hypnotist invited all the surfers on stage to have the ride of their lives. Dozens of kids went on stage including one of my friends. The hypnotist did very little to actually hypnotize the group. He just got their attention and began calming them, explaining that nothing bad was going to happen. Soon they were all under his control.

He had them sit on the stage, and then he "put them to sleep." The audience was fascinated. Here were all these kids who, just a moment before, were out of control running up to the stage, yelling and laughing, and joking that they couldn't be hypnotized; and now they all had their heads bowed and were absolutely still. Then, the hypnotist gave them the scenario. They were on the North Shore, at their most favorite break. He let them fill in the details they liked rather than imposing a detail that might cause resistance and, perhaps, break his spell. He told them that the surf was perfect; that the waves were the best they had ever seen. Again, the hypnotist only set the parameters and left the details up to the individual.

Finally, he snapped his fingers and told them they were surfing; and, they all began to surf. The audience roared with laughter as we saw our friends' concepts of how they surfed. Some were much better than they really were in the water. Others looked awkward and frustrated. The stage, their imaginary surfboard, and the imaginary waves were not giving them the experience they expected, probably because they had experienced the real thing and the illusory waves didn't measure up.

Then, the hypnotist shouted that a big set was coming, bigger than they had ever seen–a fifty-foot wave barreling towards shore. Some of the surfers panicked and paddled madly towards shore (wherever they thought shore was in their hypnotized state). Others paddled out to catch the giant wave. Some of the more frightened surfers pleaded to friends in the audience to come and help them. Some people were crying, convinced they were going to drown. The mood changed in the audience. Some took pleasure in seeing their buddies humiliated in fear. Others wondered what they could do to help. The hypnotist, sensing the change, stopped the performance, and brought everybody out of his or her hypnotized state with a snap of his fingers. Everyone grew silent as most on the stage looked dazed and tried to find a way off.

One fellow let out a giant scream. As everyone's attention went to him, he caught the fifty-foot wave and was having the ride of his life. The mood changed again. The apprehension the audience had about being voyeurs into the minds and feelings of their friends, and the discomfort that came from watching someone suffer, instantly vanished. And, the fun of the entertainment returned as we all shared in the thrill that one fellow was having riding his fifty-foot wave. He landed on the beach (the front of the stage), arms pumping in the air, and shouting in triumph, bringing the audience to its feet shouting back. Quietly the hypnotist tapped the kid on his shoulder, and he was transported from the beach to the stage. After a moment of confusion, the boy continued shouting and laughing. It might have been an illusion, but he got a thrill out of it!

The point of the story is that it would be foolish for someone *not* hypnotized to try to enter the illusion to heal it. In Goldsmith's story of the white poodle, the hypnotist had people chasing an imaginary white poodle around the stage with the task of catching it. One of the subjects saw her metaphysical practitioner in the audience and asked her to help catch the poodle. As a practitioner, if you enter the drama you have lost your perspective and prevent spiritual awareness from breaking the illusion.

When you know the omnipresence of God, you realize how ridiculous it is to try to bring God into this world to heal something. God already is here. There is only God. God is one. Everything in creation is God in manifestation. If you remember the four little words that are the heart of the Infinite Way–*is, as, one*, and *now*–you will not be tempted to change a material concept. You will stand like Jesus, in your Christhood, and treat the appearance of material power with sudden dismissal. If God *is*, what else can exist? If God appears *as* Its creation, complete and whole, what is there to ask for? Knowing that God is one, and wanting that One to fight the concept of evil, will turn you into an atheist. Realizing that God functions only in the *now* moment returns you to your Self–to that place of peace where the history of human concepts dissolves.

This is the way to live in Joy. You know that pain and suffering is illusion, not because this world is illusion but because the material concept of the spiritual reality that exists here and now is illusory. Your awareness of the Truth fills you with Joy, and because there is only One, that awareness lifts the imposition of pain from those in the scope of your consciousness. The moment you see through the appearances of material concepts, you experience the Joy that is everywhere. You feel it within yourself. Whenever I have had a spiritual realization, it fills me with joy. I almost laugh out loud. Whenever someone calls me for spiritual help, and I feel the peace come over me, I rejoice that God is omnipresent. I know that joy is an essential part of life. It comes with the freedom of knowing the non-power of the appearance world. With that attitude, you function in the world with compassion and understanding, touching those with whom you come in contact with a joy that is not attached to any human appearance. You are an instrument of God in this state of illumination.

Unconditioned Love

~

There is no fear in love;
but perfect love casts out fear.

I JOHN 4:18

Unconditioned Love completes the arch over the gate to illumination. It is the *omega* to the *alpha* of Oneness. It fulfills the circle of Christhood. It is the fulfillment of Oneness. When you enter My Kingdom, the atmosphere there is Love. It is the atmosphere in which spiritual creation exists. As fish exist in the sea, spiritual Reality exists in unconditioned Love. What does this mean as a spiritual principle? When you have completed this circle, you have cast fear out of your life. Since all spiritual principles work as one, your realization of any of the principles mentioned in this book will give you an experience of Love. When you realize the oneness of God, the feeling of release that you experience is an act of Love. God is love, and he that dwells in love dwells in God and God in him.[55]

Nothing works in this world without love. Societies fall apart without love. Families fall apart without love. Even our bodies will betray us without love. Agape, the spiritual sense of Love revealed by the Christ, falls on the just and the unjust. Agape Love can never be given or withheld.

According to the Apostle John, we love because God first loved us.[56] It seems human beings, and many in the animal kingdom, have this positive emotion called love. Could it be evidence that God is the substance of all creation? If we remember the states of being that were represented by the trinities discussed earlier, Love corresponds with the Son of God, the body, and Omnipresence. If we look at this relationship–Life-Truth-Love, Soul-Mind-Body–from a mystical perspective, we begin to see that our bodies are vehicles of Love. In Oneness, where God appears *as*, there is only One body. That body is spiritual and it is the manifestation of the infinite One in unique expression. This revelation of the body as Love comes to us, individually, in deep moments of silence where the conditioned sense of self can't enter. It is the foundation of a joyous life that is not dependent upon any material condition or situation.

We have another paradox here. We have probably all experienced love in some form in our human lives. It is an indication of spiritual activity taking place continually and universally. But, this activity–conditioned by the material sense of life and the personal sense of ego–will not lead us to spiritual freedom. In fact, many times it leads us to heartache and suffering. Yet, perfect love is an act of Grace. It casts out fear and reveals the spiritual kingdom, ever-present and *now*. How do we shift from the sense of love that brings both pleasure and pain to the fulfilling state of being that is Agape? Again, we look to the principles that take us into the realm of Spirit. We impersonalize so that we may see the Truth. We don't judge the appearance so that we remain free. We detach ourselves from concepts that limit our awareness of God. We see the non-power of the human scene and do not resist the appearance of evil. Finally, we deal with the temptations of personal power through forgiveness.

Jesus gave us two commandments: "Love God with all your heart and mind and soul; and, love your neighbor as yourself."[57] This is truly a universal principle taught all over the world in most religions. It might be stated differently, but the impulse to love is universal. How do we love God? Is it with our emotions? Is God the object of our affection? Do we expect to get pleasure from God? These questions address various natures of love, and we need to be clear that unconditioned Love is from a different state of consciousness than human love.

According to Scripture, there are three different types of love. There is *agapao*, *phileo*, and *eros*. Agapao, unconditioned Love, literally translated means charity. It loves with no conditions, no matter what. When you agapao-love, you give for the sake of making the other person happy. You truly want the best for that person, and you have no intention of receiving. Phileo, brotherly love, is based on common interests or bonds. When you phileo-love someone, it is a relationship where you give to receive–a "you scratch my back and I'll scratch yours" connection. There is still fear of being hurt in this love. Eros is erotic love or lust. It's a love based on physical appearance and sexual attraction. When you eros-love someone, you are more concerned with yourself than with the other. You expect pleasure and are disappointed when your expectation is not fulfilled. Religion has labeled these forms of love from "pure" to "degenerate." But, it excepts eros from being sinful when it is practiced in marriage between heterosexual couples. Again, we see how paradoxical love can be.

From the mystical perspective, we don't judge material appearances. The love we give is what flows through us when we are in the consciousness of God. We stay out of the battle of conflicting concepts, and see all humanity as God in expression. Conforming to dogma has never been part of mystical living. But, the human sense of right and wrong, and good and evil, is not easy to see through–even if you are with a Master. When Jesus asked Peter if he loved him, Peter couldn't commit unconditionally. Was it fear? Was it guilt? Or, is it too much to ask of a human being?

In the story in the last part of the Gospel of John, Jesus asks Peter if he loves him. Jesus is in his resurrected state, symbolizing that he is no longer subject to material conditions or material power. When he first asks Peter this question, he uses the word agapao–do you love me unconditionally? Peter answers using the word phileo–I love you as a brother. What does it take to cast out fear? It takes the death of the personal sense of ego. It takes the realization that *I am that great I am*. It takes the awareness that when I see my brother, I see myself; when I am loving my brother as myself, I am loving God. In that state of consciousness, I am truly free. Again, Jesus asks Peter the same question, and again Peter answers that he loves Jesus, but not unconditionally. What is Peter afraid of? Does he think he will be punished because he denied knowing Jesus? How many of us suffer because we are afraid to give up our human concepts (our beliefs of reward and punishment) and, because of our beliefs, never enter the circle of Christhood? Jesus was inviting Peter in, but Peter was stubborn in his beliefs. He was a rock. The third time Jesus asked the question, he used the word phileo. Peter answered that Jesus knew all things, and Jesus knew Peter loved him.

The church that Peter built was built on conditioned love; "if you do this then I will do that." At the end of the Gospel of Mark, which is considered Peter's version of Jesus' ministry, Jesus says, "He that believes and is baptized will be saved; but he that believes not shall be damned."[58] In John's gospel, Jesus urges his disciples to "Follow thou me."[59] What is it to follow Jesus? It is to love unconditionally. This is the difference between living in this world and living in My kingdom. The moment we stop judging, the moment we forgive "seventy times seven" (remember, it was Peter who asked how much we should forgive and seemed shocked at the answer), we enter My kingdom and bring into our experience the bounty of God's grace.

The act of forgiveness brings unconditioned Love into our experience. Do not think of forgiveness as pardon, or as something personal from one individual to another. This would limit forgiveness to an ego-based activity, and take it out of the realm of Spirit. Forgiveness is an activity of Grace. Forgiveness is the recognition that there is only One, not two. If we have two, then we don't have forgiveness from a spiritual base; we have pardon. We have one person trying to give to another something that in reality is spiritual, something that everybody already possesses, and something that cannot be passed one to another humanly. In its highest form, forgiveness is seeing in another his or her spiritual Self. This binds us together spiritually so that what benefits one, benefits the other. When we forgive ourselves, we forgive others. When we forgive others, we forgive ourselves. To live with a forgiving heart is to live in the bounty of God's unconditioned Love. It also brings us peace.

Individually, when we have peace in our hearts, we are peacemakers for the world. When we are at peace, we are in the atmosphere of Love. This atmosphere is the light of the world. The shadows of hatred and misunderstanding cannot exist in the light of Love. We shine this light wherever we go just by maintaining peace in our hearts.

The world has a hard time accepting the conditions for peace because most people believe in a rewarding and punishing God. Or, they believe in karmic law. What the mystical student knows is that forgiveness nullifies karma, and forgiveness brings with it the peace of God. The peace of God heals, transforms, and propels our experience out of a world of conflict into one of harmony and joy. What greater experience can we have than the peace of God? That peace brings health to our bodies. God's peace in our mind is an experience of Oneness. Peace in our family brings joy and fulfillment. Peace in our community brings progress and understanding. And, peace in the world will reveal Heaven on earth.

So, how is peace related to unconditioned Love? The answer is in the Sermon on the Mount.[60] When the Master gave this message to his disciples, he was giving them the way to live under spiritual law. The deepest parts of his sermon–"resist not evil," "love your enemies," and "pray for them who persecute you"–give you the secret for living in joy. He rejects the idea of "an eye for an eye." In a few simple instructions, the Master brings his disciples out from under the law of material cause and effect and shows them the way to Grace. If you are not grounded in spiritual principles, these instructions appear foolish. But, if you know the truth and realize the oneness of God and Its manifestation, you realize that these instructions keep you in Heaven.

FORGIVENESS

Bringing Unconditioned Love into Our Experience

Forgiveness wipes out any attachment to material appearances and the stories they carry. Lately, our public figures seem to be all about their stories. How compelling is her story? What kind of character does someone's story reveal? Unless we detach ourselves from our personal stories, we will have difficulty maintaining the clarity for spiritual manifestation. Remember, Spirit can't express Itself through the fog of human history. Calling no person on earth your parent is prerequisite to being a spiritual transparency. Being in the world but not of it is the finest paradox. On the one hand, we have only God as our father and mother. On the other, we have our human parentage and history with which we identify that links us to this world. To let go of our human history, with all of its victories and defeats, is to begin our journey on the mystical path. We are never going to spiritualize a material concept, and the moment we stop trying is our moment of freedom.

One of the great benefits of attaining mystical consciousness is living a life without fear. That freedom gives us the perspective to look at every situation that comes into our experience without reaction, and with an understanding heart. As I've said earlier about my trip on the *Tere* to the South Pacific, it was to be my spiritual initiation. Those who predicted this were right, and I learned my great lesson on this voyage. I had crossed oceans before, experienced awesome storms, and for the most part enjoyed it all without fear. On those voyages my shipmates and I were young and congenial, and we looked at the extremes of weather as an adventure. The trip to the islands of French Polynesia was another story.

Within days of leaving Honolulu we met high winds and mountainous seas that broke equipment and stressed the skipper. In addition to sailing the boat and keeping it sound, my primary purpose on board was to quell the storms and give our skipper the smooth sailing he desired. The only problem was that nobody told me I was to do this, and I actually enjoyed the excitement of the rough weather. This set a tone of resentment that polluted the atmosphere all the way to Papeete. If it hadn't been for my commitment to the owner and my inner voice reminding me that this was an initiation that I would have to complete some other time if I didn't complete it now, I would have jumped ship in Papeete and taken up an offer from acquaintances on another boat in the harbor heading for New Zealand.

Seeing the islands of Polynesia had been a childhood dream for me from the time I read Melville, London, and Stevenson. I loved the music and dancing of the islanders, and I had studied Polynesian mythology and art while at the University of Hawaii. The adventure of sailing to islands only reached by boat, and rarely visited by the outside world, thrilled me. The welcoming and loving nature of the natives warmed my heart and gave me a sense of what the early explorers must have felt when they came upon these islands after leaving a dark and gray Europe. When Gauguin showed his Tahitian paintings to the French, they did not believe his colors were truthful. They could not conceive of such colors in nature. And there I was, seeing what he saw, walking his lavender beaches, and watching brown skinned girls dressed in bright sarongs sitting on mats under shade trees. It was as if I was living in one of Gauguin's paintings! But, for every moment of pleasure and delight, there was my "Captain Bligh" waiting to discredit the experience and wanting to deny me the next.

Isn't that just like "this world?" With every bit of pleasure comes some pain. Every good carries with it a portion of evil. The coin of beauty has its ugly dark side. There was no middle path for me and I bounced from the joy of the islands to the prison of the boat. I kept a journal, which as I look back on it, became the garbage pail of my resentment. I feared having to be in the presence of a person who hated me, or at least found me thoroughly disappointing. I did not perform to his expectation and was soundly judged. I tried using the metaphysical principles I was taught as a child–denying the error and trying to find some comfort in God. But, God was nowhere to be found, and I still had another month on the boat with a long ocean crossing ahead as we made our way back to Honolulu.

How could I, who lived without fear, become so fearful? My first breakthrough came when I realized that it wasn't the person on the boat I feared. It was my own reaction to his behavior. With that realization, suddenly the hurt wasn't as deep. As we set out to cross twenty-five hundred miles of ocean, I realized for the first time that it was completely up to me to maintain my peace. I had to develop a healing consciousness and the object of the healing was myself. But, I couldn't do that if there was always me *and* something out there to be corrected. At that time, our relationship could be described as a cool politeness sparked with an occasional moment of friendship or fun. Forgiveness? It never entered my mind. My nemesis was still arrogant and demanding. If he didn't apologize, how could I forgive?

Forgiveness came the night I had the experience of the sky and sea becoming one that I told you about earlier. Everything about that night and that experience is still vivid in my mind. The incredible clearness of the stars, the heat of the night, the still ocean – all of these elements frame that experience. As part of that experience, a feeling of incredible peace came over me as I stood at the rail, my arm wrapped around a shroud as I stared out at the horizon. My personal sense of self disappeared, and the *I* that was experiencing this was the universal *I*, spiritual Being, Itself. That which was opened to me at age seventeen in the presence of Joel Goldsmith opened further to reveal that there is only One I, One presence, One cause and One effect; it is at the same time Infinite, Eternal, and Individual. Such freedom! Everything pent up in me burst out in a flood of tears that became new stars in the sea. It was all One–One body, One mind, One soul, One life, One universe, One Father-Mother God. A purging forgiveness flowed through me and left me with nothing that could react to the pettiness of human nature.

The next day harmony prevailed. The human game of ego was shut down as the whole crew experienced a reconciliation that took us beyond ego and personality, and brought us to the realization of why we set out on the voyage in the first place. It was to have been a trip celebrating love and sharing. The older generation wanted to share with the next generation the beauty and love that defined their youth in the South Seas. Everything had meaning now, and the last two weeks at sea were the most remarkable. They began with a sunset that stunned all of us with its beauty and variety of color, merging sea and sky into one blazing form. Then the winds came, fair and warm, speeding us towards home. We set every sail we carried and the boat took on a new personality, as if saying, "Look at me. Look how fast I can go!" The sea birds came around. One big old albatross soared over the boat, playing some wondrous game of tag with the masthead for a whole day. Then, as I related before, we encountered a pod of pilot whales that found our bow wake a perfect playground.

I share these experiences for a reason. They show how walking the middle path transforms your life–from one of fear and bondage to one of joy and freedom. They show that the one infinite Consciousness is universal. And, they underline how our change in perception changes our experience in life.

Non-reaction to provocation goes hand-in-hand with the absence of fear in building a healing consciousness. I discovered that being fearless on the spiritual path is not enough. A mystic must also have a healing consciousness which comes with the awareness of the spiritual dimension of life. You cannot live selfishly as a mystic, and you cannot live in a state of freedom if you do not recognize the Oneness of all creation and the inherent freedom built into God's manifestation. The sick, the poor, the abusive, and the power hungry people come into your consciousness to be freed of the limitations of material concepts. They come to you to be recognized as the Christ. If you do not recognize the spiritual nature of being in the midst of discord, disease and conflict, you will never be free of them. As you become free of the dark side of human nature, you free those who come within the scope of your consciousness. The transformation that takes place within this circle of

Oneness appears to the world as healing, and you appear to have a healing consciousness. What you really have is an awareness of the presence of God that goes before you to make the crooked places straight, and instills in you the joy that no man can take away.

ACKNOWLEDGMENTS

~

There are so many people who helped bring this book out, and I am deeply grateful to all of them for their friendship, time, and selfless contribution of their expertise.

I want to recognize Elizabeth Parker for her dedication to the Fullness of Joy. Her eye for detail and her probing questions helped to focus me on what I really wanted to say. I treasure her friendship and recognize her dedication to the Truth.

To Sandra Stephenson, my wife, always supportive and helpful, who gave many hours and her incredible spiritual insight in discerning what belonged in the book and what didn't. If the material is clear and understandable, she deserves much of the credit.

To my friend, Jerry Jampolsky, who did me the honor of reading an early draft of the book. His insight and counsel brought more joy into the book.

To Ray and Christine Wagner who have spent their lives working with writers during their careers in the movie industry. Working with them over the years has honed my writing skills, and I have benefited from their knowledge of what works and what doesn't. Thank you.

To Virginia Stephenson, my mother, who knows the Truth so well. I am blessed to have her love and support and insight. She has clarified many points of truths and helped ground this book in spiritual principle.

And, a special thanks to my family, especially Jennifer Nicholson, and her sons, Sean and Duke, for bringing so much joy into our lives.

There are so many others over the years who have supported my work and invited me to teach. It is in the consciousness of our classes–where many are joined in a common purpose of experiencing the joy of mystical union–that inspiration begins. To all of those who have joined me in this spiritual adventure, I am deeply grateful.

I would also like to thank Michael Krupp for reading the manuscript and sending it forward with such a positive endorsement, and to Gary Peattie and the people at DeVorss for their work in bringing out this book.

NOTES

1. John 14:12
2. I John 4:7
3. Philippians 2:5
4. Capitalized nouns and pronouns refer to Deity, or that spiritual state of Infinite Being.
5. Spiritual law is: "I am that I am."
6. Habakkuk 1:13
7. John 14:6
8. John 8:32
9. Matthew 7:7
10. Luke 13:24
11. John 14:6
12. John 19:11
13. 1 Corinthians 2:14

    But the natural man receiveth not the things of the Spirit of God: for they are foolishness unto him: neither can he know them, because they are spiritually dicerned.
14. Matthew 13:13-17
15. Psalms 139:8
16. Moses Maimonides, Guide of the Perplexed
17. Mary Baker Eddy, Miscellaneous Writings
18. Mark 8: 35
19. Philippians 2: 5-7
20. From "All Things Considered," NPR, March 18, 2010; interview with Andrew Cleland
21. Robert Browning (1812-1889), "Paracelsus"
22. John 17: 2-3
23. Job 19:26
24. Luke 10:27 and Mark 12:30-31
25. John 17:2-3
26. Mark 10:18 and Luke 18:19
27. Mary Baker Eddy, Science and Health, p. 203
28. John 12:32
29. John 9:3
30. Exodus 34: 7
31. The author's mother
32. The student was reported to be Albert Einstein.
33. Isaiah 11: 2-4
34. Isaiah 11:6-9
35. Joel S. Goldsmith, "The World Is New" pg. 5
36. Luke 15:31

37. John 4:32
38. Matthew 6:25-34
39. See Corinthians: 15
40. Matthew 18:18
41. Philippians 2:5
42. Joel S. Goldsmith, 1959 Hawaiian Village Class, "Living the Principles of Mysticism and Healing"
43. Matthew 5:45
44. Stanford University Memorial Chapel, Palo Alto, CA
45. John 5:31
46. John 10:30
47. Matthew 6:33
48. John 7:42
49. Psalms 24:1
50. Psalms 139:8
51. Romans 8:38-39
52. Zechariah 4:6
53. Psalms 46:10
54. Luke, Chapter 4
55. John 4:16
56. I John 4:19
57. Matthew 22:37-39
58. Mark 16:16
59. John 21:22
60. Matthew, Chapters 5-7